Contents

Welcome, and How to Use This Study Guide 5

Part 1: Things I Probably Already Knew...But Kinda Forgot

1. Sexually Set Apart—*How Sexual Holiness Is a Nonnegotiable for Disciples of Jesus* 15
2. Sex Is Spelled W-O-R-L-D-V-I-E-W—*How Our Sexual Beliefs Reveal Our Beliefs About God* 25
3. A Pretty Great Design, When Followed—*How Gender, Marriage, Sex, and Family Show Us the God We Can't See* 37
4. Demolishing Arguments, Not People—*Releasing Ideological Captives* 49

Part 2: Wait, My Kids Are Being Taught What?!

5. Are You Sex-Smarter than a Fifth Grader?—*Understanding the New National Sexual Education Standards* 63
6. The Enemy's New Playbook—*The Language and Morality of the Sexual Agenda* 77
7. The Genderbread Person—*The New Definitions of Identity, Expression, Sex, and Attraction* 87
8. Sex-Positivity—*Anything Goes If It's Consensual* 95
9. Queer Theory—*A Whole New World(view)* 107

Part 3: Things That Are Tripping Everyone Up

10. Purity Culture—*When Our Best Efforts Went Kablooey* 121

11. Pornography—*It's Not Technically Sex If You're by Yourself, Right?* 133

12. Same-Sex Attraction—*Hurting People to Be Loved* 147

13. I Identify as a [Fill in the Blank]—*Understanding Gender Identity* 163

14. *Trans*cending the Gender Cult—*When Birds Identify as Bees* 179

15. Taking Up Your Sexual Cross—*Because We're All Born That Way* 191

Notes 201

STUDY GUIDE

MAMA BEAR *Apologetics*®

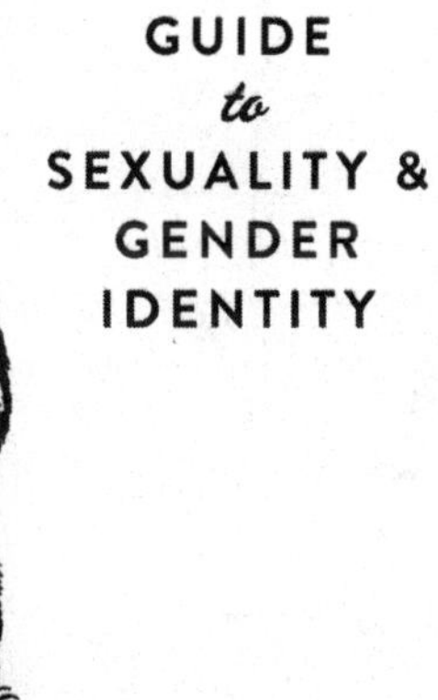

GUIDE *to* SEXUALITY & GENDER IDENTITY

HILLARY MORGAN FERRER

with TEASI CANNON

HARVEST HOUSE PUBLISHERS
EUGENE, OREGON

Published in association with the literary agency of Mark Sweeney & Associates.

Cover design by Faceout Studio

Cover illustration by Joe Hox

For bulk, special sales, or ministry purchases, please call 1-800-547-8979.
Email: CustomerService@hhpbooks.com

MAMA BEAR APOLOGETICS GUIDE TO SEXUALITY AND GENDER IDENTITY STUDY GUIDE

Published by Harvest House Publishers
Eugene, Oregon 97408
www.harvesthousepublishers.com

ISBN 978-0-7369-9093-6 (pbk)
ISBN 978-0-7369-9094-3 (eBook)

Printed in the United States of America

26 27 28 29 30 31 32 33 / BP / 10 9 8 7 6 5 4 3 2 1

Welcome, and How to Use This Study Guide

Welcome! We at Mama Bear Apologetics are so excited to share this study guide with you. Our sincere desire is that as you work through it, you will be gently challenged but not at all overwhelmed.

We love our study guides. They help us better sift through the material and digest it so we can integrate it into our everyday lives. And in *Mama Bear Apologetics Guide to Sexuality and Gender Identity*, we give a lot of practical tips for addressing these ideas with your kids. But what if we could offer you even *more* practical tips? More is better, right? (Unless you have something like scabies, and then less is generally better.)

As you read through this guide, you'll notice this icon, 🐾, which symbolizes a discipleship opportunity. With each discipleship opportunity comes an activity or conversation that will translate abstract ideas into a more concrete form so that little minds can better understand the concepts. We don't have specific ages attached to each opportunity, though we sometimes specify if the activity is for your older cubs.

Something we want everyone to keep in mind: The questions at the end of each chapter in your main book and the questions in this study guide are all applicable for dinnertime discussions! Don't assume that since you are going through these questions as an adult (or in a group of adults) that they can't be used for kids. Children from middle school on up should be able to track with the ideas presented here. So if at some point you want to grab another study guide and go through the process again with your middle schooler or high schooler, you can. And we encourage you to do so! A book doesn't have to be labeled "teen guide" to still be applicable for teens.

Challenges to identity—both through gender and sexuality—are confusing, and we cannot underestimate the impact they are having on our children. It's time to take back some ground, Mama Bears! And as we do so, remember: We don't stand before God accountable for our successes. We stand before Him accountable for our *faithfulness*. So let's be faithful in stewarding these precious boys and girls under our care.

With that in mind, here's how to make the most of your reading and this guide.

Before you read a chapter in *Mama Bear Apologetics Guide to Sexuality and Gender Identity*:

- We would love for you to have a four-color retractable click pen (flashback to high school!) on hand, but if you don't, grab four different colored pencils, pens, or highlighters and use a system similar to the one we recommend below.
- Have a dictionary or dictionary app ready for reference.
- Skim through the chapter's title and bold-print subheads to get an idea of what you're going to read. (This pre-reading strategy helps you get excited to dig in.)
- Think of a question or two you hope will be answered in the chapter.
- Pray and ask the Holy Spirit to guide you into all truth.

Lord God, our world is so broken. There is so much sexual confusion everywhere. Who am I? What can one person do? Open my eyes like the servant of Elisha, Lord. Let me see Your angels who are with me in the battle. I pray You would remove any fear I have regarding this topic and plant my feet firm in Your truth. I pray that as You shepherd me into a biblical understanding of sex and gender, that I would understand Your commandments for sex and Your design for gender. And as I understand Your commandments, Lord, help me lead my children to understand the beauty of Your magnificent design.

While you read the chapter: I have used this multicolor note-taking system for almost a decade. It has helped me to actively read and organize material so that, even years later, I can go back and glance through a book for its main points and my favorite quotes. I find that color-coding is helpful for future reference purposes. The strategy suggested here is a simplified version of my system, so you can tweak it to what works best for you.

- Black ink: Draw a box around unfamiliar words and draw a squiggly line under the definition *if* it appears within the text. (Squiggly lines will help you distinguish definitions from general notes.) If the word is not defined, record definitions in the margins or at the back of the book. We recommend looking up the definitions right away!
- Blue ink: Underline helpful passages for easy skimming. This will help you when you search through the book later for the main ideas.
- Green ink: Use this color to mark content you have questions about. (I also draw a question mark in the margin.)
- Red ink or highlight: Save this for the true "Aha!" moments or ideas you want to remember.

After you read the chapter:

- Quickly skim through the chapter to review all the words you've underlined, highlighted, and written in the margins. (Look at all those colors. This is your pat on the back for being an active reader!)
- Jump into the study guide material for that chapter.

In each chapter of the study guide, you will find an introductory thought followed by seven major sections. Because we want you to set your own pace, we haven't divided the lessons or sections into specific days; but you could choose to work through one section in a day. Here are the types of sections:

Active Reading Notes: Use this section to record a few pre-, mid-, and post-reading thoughts, including vocabulary. Here's an example.

READING FOCUS	MY RESPONSE
BEFORE YOU READ:	
After skimming the chapter title and subheads, what is one question you would like to have answered in the chapter?	My question: Why does sex matter?
WHILE YOU READ:	
List three words you discovered in the chapter, and we will add a few more words we hope you will find and look up in a dictionary.	My words: Write down words that are unfamiliar to you. Then look them up and make your best attempt at recording a brief definition. Book words: Here, you'll find words that are defined in the book. Page numbers are given so you can record the definitions in this space.

READING FOCUS	MY RESPONSE
AFTER YOU READ:	
Did you find an answer to your pre-reading question? (We hope so.) If yes, write it down.	My answer: Sex matters because it helps us see and know God accurately.
List three things you highlighted or underlined in the chapter. This can be new information you learned, encouraging reinforcements of things you already knew, or just plain anything that popped out at you.	My "Aha!" moments: 1. 2. 3.

Pick a Question: As you use this study guide, don't forget about the study questions already in the main book. Use this space as a spot to review the questions and respond to the one you find most thought-provoking.

Empowering Words: Supplemental and significant vocabulary will be given here.

Empowering Thoughts: Supplemental or reinforcing thoughts will be included here.

Digging Deeper: Here we will ask some guiding questions to help you process what you've learned and further equip you to "ROAR Like a Mother." Be aware that not all questions are asking you to simply regurgitate what the book said. Many are intended to make you *think* through the material, draw connections, and wrestle through real-life scenarios. But don't worry! If you get stuck on a question, just move on until you feel more comfortable digging in. Better yet, grab some girlfriends for coffee and discuss it! Whether or not you answer every single question, you *will* come away from this study guide with a much stronger grasp of the subject.

Key Scriptures: Here we'll offer a few related verses to help you reflect on what God says regarding the ideas presented in each chapter. We recommend journaling through each scripture, evaluating *how* the passages reinforce or address the biblical perspective of the topic at hand.

PAWS for Prayer: Here you will be guided in a sweet time of prayer—a moment to take what you're learning to God and intentionally involve the Holy Spirit in your journey. The PAWS section has four steps:

- **PRAISE**—Identify the *attributes* of God that you have seen manifested lately. You may be thankful for a recent bonus, but you will want to *praise* God for being Jehovah Rapha, the God who provides. Or maybe you didn't get the bonus and you don't know why. *Praise* God for His omniscience and how He knows what you need when you need it, even if you don't understand. Praising God for *who* He is rather than *what* He does will help orient your heart toward Him no matter what is going on in your life, good or bad. If you need a little help with this section, I recommend Googling "attributes of God" or "names of God."
- **ADMIT**—Acknowledge the areas where you have blown it. Maybe you didn't trust God, or you acted in anger with your kids or husband. Whatever your dirty laundry, bring it to God here. He already knows your heart and wants to be with you as you learn to navigate this thing called the Christian life.
- **WORSHIP through thanksgiving**—Here is where you can thank God for specific things He has *done*. When you remember that all good things come from Him, you realize you have much to be thankful for.
- **SUPPLICATION (or SUBMIT your requests)**—After you have praised God for who He is, admitted where you are struggling, and worshipped through thanksgiving, then present your requests to Him. Sometimes God doesn't give us what we ask

for because we ask with wrong motives (James 4:3). Or sometimes what we want would thwart something that He—in His goodness and knowledge—is doing in our lives that couldn't be accomplished if He answered our specific wish. But He still wants us to ask, and we can know that however He chooses to answer, it is for our good.

Don't forget! Unlike other study guides, this one has bonus discipleship content. Every time you see a , we have provided you with extra activities or conversations to have with your kids.

PART 1

Things I Probably Already Knew...But Kinda Forgot

In part 1, we learn how God defines sex and what He desires to communicate through human sexuality. We learn about the power of sex and how destructive it is when misused. We also define and explain the wonderful aspects of a biblical worldview, including how it affects the way we view sexuality. We see that an incorrect view of sex can lead to an incorrect view of God and His heart—including His good designs and His love for all humanity.

We hope the following pages will shed light on the cultural confusion you're likely experiencing related to all things sex. We also hope to empower you to have God-honoring convictions and conversations with your friends, neighbors, and children, and to find hope and peace in God's good design for His creation. Our goal is to equip you to share that hope with a hurting world in need of truth and love.

LESSON 1

Sexually Set Apart

How Sexual Holiness Is a Nonnegotiable for Disciples of Jesus

God's commands regarding sex are not just a side issue. They are a prominent theme spanning the Old and New Testaments, especially in terms of holiness. The word *holy* literally means "set apart for a special purpose." As Christians, our sexual ethic is a major way in which we are called to be set apart from the world because sexual holiness is, in essence, a sign of our knowledge of and commitment to God. It has always been this way.

—*Mama Bear Apologetics Guide to Sexuality and Gender Identity*, pages 25–26

ACTIVE READING NOTES

READING FOCUS	MY RESPONSE
BEFORE YOU READ:	
After skimming the chapter title and subheads, what is one question you would like to have answered in the chapter?	My question:
WHILE YOU READ:	
List three words you discovered in the chapter in addition to the words we have provided.	My words: Book words: *postmodernism* (page 24)— *holy* (page 26)— *the argument from silence* (page 28)— *covenant* (page 32)—

READING FOCUS	MY RESPONSE
AFTER YOU READ:	
Did you find an answer to your pre-reading question? (We hope so.) If yes, write it down.	My answer:
List three things you highlighted or underlined in the chapter. This can be new information you learned, encouraging reinforcements of things you already knew, or just plain anything that popped out at you.	My "Aha!" moments: 1. 2. 3.

PICK A QUESTION

Use this space to review the study questions at the end of the chapter and respond to the one you find most thought-provoking or convicting.

EMPOWERING WORDS

- *Argument from silence*—Drawing a conclusion based on what isn't said, rather than what is said. Example: One kid telling another, "Well, nobody ever said we couldn't [insert whatever wild thing they want to do that it never occurred to you to prohibit]."
- *Sufficiency of Scripture*—Scripture contains all the words God intended His people to have at each stage of redemptive history, and it now contains what we need to know for salvation and trusting and obeying God perfectly (Deuteronomy 29:29).
- *Perspicuity (clarity) of Scripture*—According to this doctrine, you don't need a seminary degree to understand what God has said to you and what He wants for your life. The Bible's teachings can be understood by all who read it to seek God's help (Deuteronomy 6:6-7).
- *Sin*—Any failure to conform to the moral law of God in act, attitude, or nature.
- *Sanctification*—The maturation process of a Christian whereby they progressively become more like Christ in heart, words, and action. Unlike the gift of salvation, the sanctifying process involves hard work, obedience, and our active and mindful participation.

EMPOWERING THOUGHTS

In this chapter we learn that *holiness* literally means "set apart for a special purpose." On page 26, we read that one of the defining characteristics of Christ's followers is sexual holiness. While sexual holiness is a significant defining characteristic of Christ-followers and reflects essential truths to those around us, we must remember it's not the primary purpose of the gospel or the ultimate goal of the Christian life.

Read the following verses and record what they say about our primary goal as followers of Christ.

Philippians 3:10-12:

Hebrews 13:21:

 *What Does It Mean to Be Set Apart?*

What items do you have lying around your home or office that are set apart for special use? A LEGO set? A special dress? Video game controllers? What about things that have a particular use and would be ruined were you to misuse them? (Like contacts. You can't really use contacts for anything other than seeing. And if you do...well, you probably shouldn't put them back in your eyes!) Start creating this category in your child's mind so they have examples to draw from when you discuss that they as a Christian are to be holy—set apart for a special use.

DIGGING DEEPER

1. Read the paragraph that starts by describing the Asherah poles on page 27. What can we learn about the character and motives of the pagan gods from the type of worship they required?

How is that different from the God of the Bible?

2. In the first paragraph of the section called "The New Testament: Pointing Back to God's Design" on page 28, we are introduced to a common misinterpretation regarding Jesus's views on sexuality, especially homosexuality. This view asserts that because Jesus doesn't explicitly condemn homosexuality, it must be condoned—at least in some measure. How is the argument from silence logically fallacious and theologically dangerous? What other kinds of things could we theoretically consider permissible if our only criteria for what's impermissible is something that's explicitly forbidden by Jesus?

3. Read the verses listed on pages 29-30. How would you respond to a self-identified Christian who claims that Christians who reject other sexual expressions or orientations are misrepresenting God's heart, or promoting harmful doctrines that hurt and marginalize people whom God has called us to love? (Pay special attention to the Thessalonians passage.)

4. A covenant is a promise that is ratified and remembered by something external. Use pages 32–33 to help you fill in the chart below highlighting several covenants in the Bible.

COVENANT/ WITH WHOM	PROMISE	PHYSICAL/ EXTERNAL SIGN
Noahic		
Abrahamic		
Marriage		

5. How might understanding sex as an act of repeating marital vows in bodily form change the way people view sex, even within a marriage? How might it change the way husbands approach or respond to their wives during intimate moments? What about wives to their husbands?

6. How is fire a useful analogy for explaining the boundaries regarding sex (pages 34–35)?

Name some other teaching examples you could use with your kids:

- Things so powerful they need boundaries

- Things so valuable they need protection

7. How does the Christian view of sex reflect a heightened value on human beings and their bodies?

Keeping It Simple

This is where you can have some fun. Pick something random in your house—such as orange juice or a spatula—and then remind your kids constantly throughout the week everything it's *not* to be used for (such as washing the dog, waxing the car, or cleaning up vomit). Have them join in; I bet they'll be even more creative than you! When they've had about all they can take, ask them, "We had some fun with that, but do you think our extra instructions regarding [fill in the blank] were helpful? Stupid? Necessary? Unnecessary?"

Bring it back to God's Word and sexuality. The Bible doesn't claim to be an exhaustive book, detailing everything *not* to do. Instead, it provides us with a clear original design (Genesis 5:2), the original purpose of sex (Genesis 1:28; 2:23-25), and a few examples of people misusing His good gift of sexuality (Leviticus 18; 20). If your kids ever ask if an alternate sexuality or gender is a sin, simply respond with: "What was God's original design?" Keep it simple.

KEY SCRIPTURES

We encourage you to read the following verses in context (meaning, read at least the entire chapter). Reflect on how they relate to what you're learning, and thank God for the hope and guidance found in His Word.

- 2 Timothy 2:21: "If anyone cleanses himself from what is dishonorable, he will be a vessel for honorable use, set apart as holy, useful to the master of the house, ready for every good work."
- Hebrews 10:26 (NIV): "If we deliberately keep on sinning after we have received the knowledge of the truth, no sacrifice for sins is left." (This whole chapter is amazing.)
- Romans 12:2: "Do not be conformed to this world, but be transformed by the renewal of your mind, that by testing you may discern what is the will of God, what is good and acceptable and perfect."

PAWS FOR PRAYER

In closing this chapter, reflect on what you learned in lesson 1 and journal your prayer to God here:

Praise:

Admit:

Worship with thanksgiving:

Supplication (submit your requests):

LESSON 2

Sex Is Spelled W-O-R-L-D-V-I-E-W

How Our Sexual Beliefs Reveal Our Beliefs About God

While many Christians think of sexuality as only a moral issue, the implications are much more complex. A person's core view of sexuality isn't just tied to their view of God, but to their entire worldview...Since both sex and gender existed before the fall, then they are inherently good! Sex doesn't just feel good; it is *morally good* when used according to God's design! And gender differences were part of God's original design. When we reject the concept of male and female, we tell the world that God's created order isn't good.

—*Mama Bear Apologetics Guide to Sexuality and Gender Identity*, pages 42, 45

ACTIVE READING NOTES

READING FOCUS	MY RESPONSE
BEFORE YOU READ:	
After skimming the chapter title and subheads, what is one question you would like to have answered in the chapter?	My question:
WHILE YOU READ:	
List three words you discovered in the chapter in addition to the words we have provided.	My words: Book words: *teleology* (page 46)— *telos* (page 46)—
AFTER YOU READ:	
Did you find an answer to your pre-reading question? (We hope so.) If yes, write it down.	My answer:

READING FOCUS	MY RESPONSE
List three things you highlighted or underlined in the chapter. This can be new information you learned, encouraging reinforcements of things you already knew, or just plain anything that popped out at you.	My "Aha!" moments: 1. 2. 3.

PICK A QUESTION

Use this space to review the study questions at the end of the chapter and respond to the one you find most thought-provoking or convicting.

EMPOWERING WORDS

- *Epistemology*—The study of how we gain knowledge. It engages questions like, "What is knowledge?" and "How is knowledge acquired?"
- *Moral relativism*—An ideology that suggests there is no universal or absolute set of moral principles, but that moral standards

are defined by people according to their time, place, and context, and cannot be objectively determined.

- *General revelation*—The truths that can be known about God through His creation (Romans 1:20).
- *Special revelation*—Knowledge about God that cannot be revealed through nature, but requires direct revelation through miraculous means, including the written Word of God, and, most importantly, Jesus Christ.
- *Justification*—The legal act of God in which He considers our sins forgiven and applies Christ's righteousness to us.
- *Glorification*—When Christ returns and gives all believers—alive and dead—perfect resurrected bodies like His own, we will be glorified.

EMPOWERING THOUGHTS

One of the best reasons to have an accurate worldview is so life doesn't take you by surprise. We expect that living the Christian life will be hard. We expect our desires to wage war against what the Lord has called us to do. We expect that staying faithful to Christ will sometimes put us on the outs with society. We expect spiritual attacks, trials, tribulations, and suffering. We expect others to behave selfishly. We expect to have to discipline our children, and we expect raising them well will be hard work because we have to overcome their already-present sin nature. Take some time to thank God for the way He has accurately described reality through Scripture and prepared you for every hardship that is coming your way. And thank Him again that our destiny is to one day be with Him forever, where every hardship will cease.

1. Some well-meaning Christian books take every single positive message in Scripture and then label it as a "promise" from God. How could misunderstanding the "promises of God" actually lead

you toward a more difficult life, in terms of what you expect from reality?

2. Have you ever been blindsided by something you thought God had "promised" you freedom from? How does having an accurate worldview protect you from unnecessary heartache?

DIGGING DEEPER

In this chapter we learn how to understand a worldview by looking at several analogies. Look through the five analogies discussed on pages 42–43, and record what each analogy teaches about the significance and function of a worldview by answering the following questions:

A WORLDVIEW IS LIKE... (ANALOGY)	WORLDVIEW FUNCTION
A Lens	How does a well-oriented worldview help us see accurately?
Rules to a Game	How is a worldview like the rules to a game?

A WORLDVIEW IS LIKE... (ANALOGY)	WORLDVIEW FUNCTION
A Filter	What should a good worldview allow in and keep out?
A Puzzle Box Top	How does knowing what a biblical worldview is supposed to look like help our kids?
A Cartographer's Map	How does a good worldview help us navigate where we are, how we got there, where we want to be, and what obstacles to expect?

1. Take a look at the questions a worldview answers as listed on pages 45–50. How do the answers to these questions change depending on whether God or humans are the foundation of truth and reality? (You'll really have to think through this! This isn't the kind of question to try to regurgitate!)

WORLDVIEW STATEMENT	SUMMARIZE IN YOUR OWN WORDS	IMPLICATIONS FOR SEXUALITY
God Himself is the foundation of ____________ and ____________.		
Ultimate truth is ____________, not ____________.		
Humans are uniquely created in the ____________ of ____________.		
God created with ____________.		
God's ____________ law is part of our ____________.		
____________ got us all confused.		

WORLDVIEW STATEMENT	SUMMARIZE IN YOUR OWN WORDS	IMPLICATIONS FOR SEXUALITY
We cannot be reconciled to our _________ until we are reconciled to _____ through ___________.		
Not everything is ___________...yet.		

2. The concept of teleology is important to every facet of human existence, especially in understanding the role of a Christian and our identity in Christ. Describe in your own words what teleology is and why it is important to understand.

- What is the telos of a pair of scissors?
- Of a Crock-Pot?
- Of a duck's webbed feet?
- Of a human?
- Of a Christian?

3. A telos also determines what is within an organism's nature. Have you ever seen an animal that was not allowed to act like an animal? A dog that was always chained up? A horse that never left a small pen? How does flourishing decline when animals are not allowed to fulfill their telos? What about a dog who didn't *want* to run around? How can rejecting a telos be a symptom that a creature is unhealthy?

4. According to points 4, 5, and 7 on pages 46–47, 49–50, why would we *expect* a kind of peace when obeying God? How does the truth that not everything is redeemed *yet* (see page 50) prepare us to wage a war against our natural inclinations to find this peace? How do these two seemingly contradictory points match what we experience in reality?

5. On page 51, we read, "We humbly accept Christ as the only One who can restore us to what humans were intended to be, and we have faith that living according to His design will bring us the ultimate freedom, even if our desires disagree for a time." What are some desires you have had to relinquish in your pursuit of living according to God's design?

6. How does understanding the way our bodies were created inform how we treat our bodies? How does *ignoring* the way we were created show disrespect for God as Creator?

7. Read the section titled "You *Was*, Not You *Is*." What is the danger in using "I am" statements that differ from our identity in Christ? What are some "I am" statements you have been tempted to speak over yourself that contradict who Christ says you are? What are some proper "I am" statements to combat these? (For example, "I am gay" can become "I struggle with same-sex attraction.")

KEY SCRIPTURES

We encourage you to read the following verses in context (meaning, read at least the entire chapter). Reflect on how they relate to what you're learning, and thank God for the hope and guidance found in His Word.

- 1 Corinthians 6:11: "Such were some of you. But you were washed, you were sanctified, you were justified in the name of the Lord Jesus Christ and by the Spirit of our God."
- Romans 7:15: "I do not understand my own actions. For I do not do what I want, but I do the very thing I hate."

- Colossians 2:13: "You, who were dead in your trespasses and the uncircumcision of your flesh, God made alive together with him, having forgiven us all our trespasses."
- Psalm 40:4: "Blessed is the man who makes the LORD his trust, who does not turn to the proud, to those who go astray after a lie!"

PAWS FOR PRAYER

In closing this chapter, reflect on what you learned in lesson 2 and journal your prayer to God here:

Praise:

Admit:

Worship with thanksgiving:

Supplication (submit your requests):

LESSON 3

A Pretty Great Design, When Followed

How Gender, Marriage, Sex, and Family Show Us the God We Can't See

Gender, sex, marriage, and family matter because they were intended to show us the God we can't see. Even more, they point the world to the God they cannot see in hopes that what is invisible can become more understandable. Any movement seeking to destroy gender, sex, marriage, or family is destroying the message God intended, the picture He gave us in order to understand Him. And that picture is a pretty great design… *when followed.*

—*Mama Bear Apologetics Guide to Sexuality and Gender Identity*, page 72

ACTIVE READING NOTES

READING FOCUS	MY RESPONSE
BEFORE YOU READ:	
After skimming the chapter title and subheads, what is one question you would like to have answered in the chapter?	My question:
WHILE YOU READ:	
List three words you discovered in the chapter in addition to the words we have provided.	My words: Book words: *ontology* (page 61)— *functional hierarchy* (page 61)— *imago dei* (page 66)—
AFTER YOU READ:	
Did you find an answer to your pre-reading question? (We hope so.) If yes, write it down.	My answer:

READING FOCUS	MY RESPONSE
List three things you highlighted or underlined in the chapter. This can be new information you learned, encouraging reinforcements of things you already knew, or just plain anything that popped out at you.	My "Aha!" moments: 1. 2. 3.

PICK A QUESTION

Use this space to review the study questions at the end of the chapter and respond to the one you find most thought-provoking or convicting.

EMPOWERING WORDS

- *Communicable attributes of God*—Attributes of God that we, as humans, can reflect, such as faithfulness, truthfulness, mercy, goodness, justice, love, grace, and holiness.
- *Incommunicable attributes of God*—God also has unique characteristics, such as immutability (unchangingness), eternality, omnipresence, omniscience, and aseity (self-origination).
- *Covenant*—A sacred, unchangeable, and binding agreement

exists between God and humanity that stipulates the conditions of our relationship.

- *Subordinationism*—The heresy that states the Son is *ontologically inferior* to the Father (not to be confused with the historic biblical teaching that the Son is *functionally* subordinate to the Father while on earth).

EMPOWERING THOUGHTS

One of the beautiful things about God is that He doesn't ask us to do anything He wasn't willing to do first. Read Luke 2. God was born. He learned obedience (Hebrews 5:8). He submitted to His parents. He grew in wisdom. He asked questions. He suffered. And He placed Himself under the authority of God, becoming obedient to the point of death (Philippians 2). How might this fact change our ideas of what we are owed, what our rights are, or how we ought to view authority?

DIGGING DEEPER

1. In this chapter we touch on biblical authority and address some of the perversions and broken examples that hinder our submission to God's design. On page 56, we learn that willing and even joyful submission to God's design is possible when we understand God's goodness and trust in His love. How might those with broken examples of authority overcome past trauma and learn to trust in God's goodness?

2. What kind of authority figures have you experienced in your own life? Were they easy or hard to follow? Have you ever noticed yourself

interacting with God in a similar way as you interacted with your earthly authority figures?

3. What is the difference between *functional* hierarchy and *ontological* hierarchy? Give examples.

4. Review the passage on authority within the Godhead on pages 61–64. How do we see functional hierarchy (sometimes called functional order) modeled within the Godhead, and what makes it function so smoothly?

5. Christ *chose* submission to the Father when He became human. Similarly, we women *choose* who we are going to submit to when we decide to become wives. If becoming a wife means choosing under whose authority to put oneself, how might that affect the way we train our girls to pick husbands?

6. In our fallen world, how have you seen authority and submission warped to imply inequality between parties? Is that how the Bible views authority? How has this misunderstanding of authority affected the way some men have treated their wives? Explain, in your own words, why it is so important for us as Christians to correctly understand the concept of authority.

 *Understanding the Importance of Representing God Well*

Review the fashion analogy on pages 65–66. What are your kids most proud of? Their football prowess? Their artistic skills? Have them imagine that a college scout is coming to evaluate them to decide if they are going to get a full-ride scholarship or an amazing opportunity based on their performance. Now have them imagine that someone else either puts their name on your child's artwork or wears your child's jersey and performs horribly. How would they feel? Angry? Betrayed? When we misrepresent God through our sex lives, we are misrepresenting Him to the world. How might this tangible example help your kids understand why representing God well through our sexuality is so important?

7. In the space below, summarize in one or two sentences the message God intends to send through each of the following:

    a. The message of gender (page 66):

b. The message of marriage (pages 66–67):

c. The message of sex (pages 67–68):

d. The message of family (pages 68–69):

8. Each message reflects a picture. For example, the message of gender paints a picture of the image of God. In the space below, describe how secularism has warped each message. What might be the ramifications of these warped worldviews on our human understandings of God? (Feel free to get creative here.)

   a. The secular message of gender: Gender is just ______________

   ____

   ____

If taken as a picture of God, this misunderstanding might depict God as ______________________________

____

____

b. The secular message of marriage: Marriage is just ____________

____

____

If taken as a picture of God, this misunderstanding might depict God as ______________________________

____

____

c. The secular message of sex: Sex is just ____________

____

____

If taken as a picture of God, this misunderstanding might depict God as ______________________________

____

____

d. The secular message of family: Family is just ____________

____

____

If taken as a picture of God, this misunderstanding might depict God as ______________________________

____

____

9. On page 70, we read, "Like all things, we need balance. We cannot elevate God's good design to the point where people who have missed it feel like they are forever on the outs. And we cannot elevate God's redemption to the point where people feel like there's a get-out-of-jail-free card whenever things get tough."

   Almost everyone tends to emphasize one trait over the other—God's wrath and God's love, God's design and God's redemption. Which characteristics do you gravitate toward?

10. On page 71, we read, "We cannot stop lifting up God's design as the ideal, even if we haven't attained it." Why is this true?

    Consider a coach, leader, or teacher who has influenced and led others to excellence despite his or her own imperfections. How can this example encourage us to lovingly reinforce God's design with our children even if we have fallen short in our own lives?

KEY SCRIPTURES

We encourage you to read the following verses in context (meaning, read at least the entire chapter). Reflect on how they relate to what you're learning, and thank God for the hope and guidance found in His Word.

- Romans 2:4: "Do you presume on the riches of his kindness

and forbearance and patience, not knowing that God's kindness is meant to lead you to repentance?"

- Hebrews 4:16: "Let us then with confidence draw near to the throne of grace, that we may receive mercy and find grace to help in time of need."
- 1 Corinthians 10:31: "Whether you eat or drink, or whatever you do, do all to the glory of God."
- Ecclesiastes 12:13: "The end of the matter; all has been heard. Fear God and keep his commandments, for this is the whole duty of man."

PAWS FOR PRAYER

In closing this chapter, reflect on what you learned in lesson 3 and journal your prayer to God here:

Praise:

Admit:

Worship with thanksgiving:

Supplication (submit your requests):

LESSON 4

Demolishing Arguments, Not People

Releasing Ideological Captives

Jesus dealt with ideas forcefully and without apology. He also dealt with individuals according to their need: What was keeping the person from unifying with the heart and mind of God? We should model our approach after Jesus. We don't just answer questions; we answer *people* (Colossians 4:6). There is a time to demolish arguments and a time to love a person tangled in a thornbush of bad ideas. Ultimately, we need to teach our kids how to manage both.

—*Mama Bear Apologetics Guide to Sexuality and Gender Identity*, page 86

ACTIVE READING NOTES

READING FOCUS	MY RESPONSE
BEFORE YOU READ:	
After skimming the chapter title and subheads, what is one question you would like to have answered in the chapter?	My question:
WHILE YOU READ:	
List three words you discovered in the chapter in addition to the words we have provided.	My words: Book words: *deductive reasoning* (page 80)— *incoherent* (page 81)— *grounding problem* (page 81)— *emotional reasoning* (page 83)—

READING FOCUS	MY RESPONSE
AFTER YOU READ:	
Did you find an answer to your pre-reading question? (We hope so.) If yes, write it down.	My answer:
List three things you highlighted or underlined in the chapter. This can be new information you learned, encouraging reinforcements of things you already knew, or just plain anything that popped out at you.	My "Aha!" moments: 1. 2. 3.

PICK A QUESTION

Use this space to review the study questions at the end of the chapter and respond to the one you find most thought-provoking or convicting.

EMPOWERING WORDS

- *Emotionalism*—Prioritizing our feelings over our God-given reasoning faculties.
- *Judgment*—Assessing a situation and drawing conclusions based on one's perception of truth and reality.
- *Reason*—The ability of the mind to think, understand, and support thoughts and conclusions through logic.
- *Hermeneutics*—The study of the principles and methods of interpreting the biblical text.
- *Grounding problem*—When one accepts a concept without a bedrock truth to support it. For example: Could something (or someone) have an intentional and purposeful design without a designer?

EMPOWERING THOUGHTS

One of the most frequently asked questions we get at Mama Bear Apologetics is on how to prepare one's kids for loving same-sex attracted or gender-confused family and friends without introducing them to concepts that are too mature for them to understand. So here's one of the activities we recommend called "Playing the Image of God."

Your children know they're special to you, but do they know they are special just by being human? They are! Because they are created *in the image of God*. Now, your job is to show them that every person is a fellow image bearer. Whenever you're out and about, or whenever you're talking about another person, make sure to ask, "Is that person made in the image of God?" (Don't forget to add questions about things *not* made in the image of God—such as a cute puppy, a really good candy bar, or a squirrel. Fabulous as those are, they are not created in the image of God the way humans are.) Maybe the person has differently colored hair or skin from your family. Maybe she's differently abled, or maybe he's dressed like a clown. Maybe it's a baby in the womb! No matter how that person looks or acts, remind your kids that *all* humans are created in the image of God and thus have inherent worth and value. (We used to say "dignity and respect," but that phrase has gotten so hijacked that we are sticking with "worth and value" now because it is clearer.)

Once the category "made in the image of God to be treated with worth and value" is firmly connected to all humans, let's get a little more nuanced. Create in their mind a second set of categories: actions that do or do not reflect the image of God. As humans we are all *created* in God's image, but we can make decisions that do not *reflect* His image. Did a person's theft reflect God's image? No. Was the person who yelled at someone on the highway reflecting God's image? No. Even when you discipline your kids, remind them, "This does not change your standing as an image bearer of God. However, your actions were disobedient. You did not reflect that image. There will be consequences for your behavior." This makes the category personal, showing how even they—your darlings—can poorly reflect God's image. Yet no matter their behavior, nothing can change their identity as image bearers of God.

As you have this conversation day after day, year after year, it will be easier to introduce societal behaviors (especially those pertaining to sexuality) that do not reflect God's design. Children will already know that a person's actions have no bearing on whether the individual is made in the image of God and has inherent worth and value. They will be able to distinguish between *identity* and *behavior*. Remind them that while some people choose to identify themselves by their behavior, that is not how we as Christians will identify them.

In the main book's chapter, we look at four categories that can help us to love people well, and to maintain relationships without compromising truth. Share a personal takeaway from each category below:

1. Is This a Person or an Idea? (page 77)

____

2. An Enemy with No Scruples (pages 77–80)

---

3. Loving God by Loving Truth (pages 80–84)

---

4. Embracing Our Inner Warrior Bear and Nurturing Bear (pages 84–86)

DIGGING DEEPER

1. Read pages 75–77. What do you think is the difference between a rebel and a captive? Why do you think this is an important distinction?

2. Describe how today's cultural sexual ideologies are like getting caught in a thornbush.

3. How does a false definition of love (i.e., celebrating unbiblical expressions of gender or sexuality) damage a person's Christian worldview? (See pages 78–79.)

4. What is the proper way to love God and love others? (See pages 79–80.)

5. Why do you think truth is so necessary for biblical love and a biblical worldview (John 4:24; 14:6; 1 John 4:8)?

6. If God (the Divine Mind) doesn't exist, not only is human life purposeless; it's also objectively worthless. Think of one or two other human values that suffer the "grounding problem" without God. (See pages 80–81.)

   •

   •

7. Read pages 80–84 on logical and emotional reasoning. Then go to https://mamabearapologetics.com/logic-worksheet/ to download the worksheet booklet. See if you can complete a few of the logic questions. What is the main difference between *logical* reasoning and *emotional* reasoning? (Hint: Emotional reasoning relies on what universal assumption?)

8. Jesus used different approaches when He spoke to crowds versus when He spoke to individuals. What would you say was the main difference?

   How can you apply His example to your own life?

   What are some possible repercussions if we get these two tactics backward? That is, what if we speak to individuals the way Jesus spoke to crowds, and what if we speak to crowds the way He spoke to individuals?

 *When Needs Affect Behaviors*

Consider the times when your kids act out in disobedience. Sometimes their behavior is simply rebellion, but sometimes it stems from an unmet need or being exhausted at the end of a hard day. Consequences should always follow inappropriate behavior, but sometimes the deeper needs ought to be addressed first. Is your daughter overwhelmed by outside stimuli? Maybe she needs a bubble bath before you discuss the consequences of her actions. Is your son acting out of frustration over a social or family situation? Sometimes healthy comfort food will help him relax enough to discuss his actions. In both these examples, we are addressing our children's deeper needs with grace before launching into correction mode.

Digging into Logic

On pages 80–83, we go through some basic argument structures. For the purposes of this book, we use three categories of statements. What categories do these letters stand for?

A: ______________________________

FC: ______________________________

C: ______________________________

Fill in the blank for this statement (see page 82):

> Assumptions need to be ______________, and fact claims need to be ______________. If either of those is incorrect, then the conclusion is usually incorrect. But until you uncover the logic, it's just two people ______________ ________ __________
> ____________.

Example: Imagine you are talking with someone who keeps talking about the oppressive nature of gender differences. You grant that oppression from gender can exist but disagree that all gender differences are oppressive. The person gives you example after example of gender inequalities.

Circle which of the following statements the person *thinks* you are disagreeing with:

Assumption: All inequalities come down to power and oppression.

Fact Claim: There is gender inequality.

Conclusion: Gender differences are oppressive.

Put a box around the statement you are *actually* disagreeing with. How does this illustrate two people talking past each other?

KEY SCRIPTURES

We encourage you to read the following verses in context (meaning, read at least the entire chapter). Reflect on how they relate to what you're learning, and thank God for the hope and guidance found in His Word.

- Mark 10:27: "With man it is impossible, but not with God. For all things are possible with God."
- John 14:15: "If you love me, you will keep my commandments."
- Hebrews 10:17: "I will remember their sins and their lawless deeds no more."
- Matthew 10:34: "Do not think that I have come to bring peace to the earth. I have not come to bring peace, but a sword."

Learn the Prayer of Saint Francis with your children:

Lord, make me an instrument of Your peace.
Where there is hatred, let me sow love.
Where there is injury, let me bring pardon.
Where there is doubt, let me bring faith.
Where there is despair, let me bring hope.
Where there is darkness, let me bring Your light.
Where there is sadness, let me bring joy.

O divine Master, let me not seek as much
to be consoled as to console,
to be understood as to understand,
to be loved as to love,
for it is in giving that we receive,
it is in pardoning that we are pardoned,
and it is in dying that we are born to everlasting life.

PAWS FOR PRAYER

In closing this chapter, reflect on what you learned in lesson 4 and journal your prayer to God here:

Praise:

Admit:

Worship with thanksgiving:

Supplication (submit your requests):

PART 2

Wait, My Kids Are Being Taught What?!

A worldview is the lens through which you perceive the world around you. It affects how you interpret your lived experiences and how you draw conclusions about how the world works. It influences what you do with all the puzzle pieces life throws your way and how you answer life's most significant questions: What does it mean to be human? Why are we here? Where did we come from? What is wrong with the world? How can it be fixed? Where are we headed? What is true "human flourishing"?

The biblical worldview is both cohesive and in line with reality. It stands apart from other worldviews in that—when properly understood—it can be applied to life's big questions. The biblical worldview does not contradict itself, and it leads to a society that is orderly and safe. It also results in hope, peace, and objectively verifiable answers.

In part 2, we will learn about the unbiblical worldview that is guiding the mission and values behind some of the confusing and dangerous sexual guidelines influencing public education and secular thought today. We will witness *linguistic theft* at work again as we look beneath the surface of the sexual agenda that seeks to tempt our kids with nice-sounding concepts, subtly (and sometimes not so subtly) pulling them outside the God-glorifying boundaries intended to protect and bless them.

This section offers several practical steps parents can take toward greater awareness and advice on how to be salt and light to our local government, schools, and communities as we walk in respect without compromising on truth.

LESSON 5

Are You Sex-Smarter than a Fifth Grader?

Understanding the New National Sexual Education Standards

Instead of sex education being about puberty and reproduction, it is now about exploring *who* you want to have sex with.[1] And only you can decide that for yourself...Experimenting with different orientations is being taught as a normal part of sexual development...We must remember that [these] practices and procedures don't just come out of thin air. They come from an ideological background, which, in turn, stems from a worldview—how a person perceives reality and what they think needs to happen in order to improve the world. There is an end goal in mind...If you don't understand the worldview behind the policies, you'll find yourself unable to see the pattern that is emerging, the picture that is created from putting all these little puzzle pieces together.

—*Mama Bear Apologetics Guide to Sexuality and Gender Identity*, pages 96, 97

ACTIVE READING NOTES

READING FOCUS	MY RESPONSE
BEFORE YOU READ:	
After skimming the chapter title and subheads, what is one question you would like to have answered in the chapter?	My question:
WHILE YOU READ:	
List three words you discovered in the chapter in addition to the words we have provided.	My words: Book words: *NSES* (page 92)— *sexual risk avoidance* (page 93)— *sexual risk reduction* (page 93)— *sexual autonomy* (page 95)— *marginalize* (page 99)—

AFTER YOU READ:	
Did you find an answer to your pre-reading question? (We hope so.) If yes, write it down.	My answer:
List three things you highlighted or underlined in the chapter. This can be new information you learned, encouraging reinforcements of things you already knew, or just plain anything that popped out at you.	My "Aha!" moments: 1. 2. 3.

PICK A QUESTION

Use this space to review the study questions at the end of the chapter and respond to the one you find most thought-provoking or convicting.

EMPOWERING WORDS

- *Ontology*—A branch of philosophy that seeks the classification and explanation of essence, being, and existence.
- *Sociology*—The study of the development, structure, and functioning of human society and social problems.
- *Anthropology*—The study of humanity through the application of biology, cultural studies, archaeology, linguistics, and other social sciences.
- *Theology*—The study of the nature of God.
- *Remnant*—God has always reserved for Himself a group of people who are faithful in deed, not just in word, no matter how culture changes around them. This doctrine says they will ultimately experience the fulfillment of God's promises (1 Kings 19:18; Zephaniah 3:9-20; Revelation 12:17).

EMPOWERING THOUGHTS

The Christian worldview helps us understand and accept the reality we see around us—both the good and bad—while also explaining why we intuitively know that things are not the way they are supposed to be. One of the most important parts of the Christian worldview is our view of eternal life and the fact that this world is not our true home! All the injustices, all the suffering, all the crime, and all the unhealthiness will ultimately be dealt with, *and not by us.* By following the commands of Jesus, we create little ripples around us that point to the kingdom that will one day be our home. But we are not responsible for making the entire world a utopian reality in the here and now. We live at the nexus of freedom and empowerment: freedom to rest in God's sovereignty while—at the same time—being empowered to cultivate the environment around us for the glory of God. Selah, y'all.

 *From Fun to Anarchy in Less Than an Hour*

Grab a board game or a card game your family plays frequently. Then tell your kids that this time, there's a new rule: *Anyone* can make *any* new rule, *whenever* they want. For instance, if yellow is about to win, blue can declare that blue is now allowed to switch places with any other player on the board. The game might start out with laughter, but be sure to step in before your children throttle each other.

Once you're finished playing, ask your kids: How much harder was it to play the game? While it might have been fun for a little while to make up the rules, did the fun last? Use this as an illustration about why *we need rules that don't change*, and why they should come from an outside party (like God). Without set rules, anyone *in* the game will try to change the rules *in their own favor.*

DIGGING DEEPER

1. In this chapter we are introduced to the National Sex Education Standards (NSES) coming to a school near you. On page 93, we learn what steps we can take to become more informed and engaged in what's going on at a local level. In the spaces below, describe each of those steps:

   Step one: Gather ______________________________

   ____

   Step two: Contact ______________________________

   ____

   Step three: Find out ______________________________

   ____

   Step four: Ask ______________________________

   ____

2. If, after researching, we have objections, what is the proper chain of communication we should try to follow (page 94)?

   First contact: ______________________________

   Second contact: ______________________________

   Third contact: ______________________________

   Fourth contact: ______________________________

3. Why should we keep good records and paper trails of our conversations?

   And remember, our actions can speak louder than words. We want to be salt and light.

4. Have you ever brought an objection to one of your children's teachers (maybe even at church)? In what ways did you use (or fail to use) grace and discernment?

5. What are some things you can do today to build a relational bridge with the teachers, principals, and school boards in your community?

6. What three factors make up a "healthy" relationship according to the NSES (page 95)?

    - ______________________________
    - ______________________________
    - ______________________________

7. From the perspective of sex-positivity, the goal is to help kids become familiar with their sexual identity by way of exploring all the options (pages 95–96).

    a. What is God's goal for our children's sexuality? (See 1 Thessalonians 4:3-5.)

    b. What does the Bible say about our wants? (See Colossians 3:5.)

    c. What does the Bible say about our needs? (See Matthew 6:25-34.)

d. Not all explorations end well. List at least two potentially life-altering consequences of sexual exploration.

Experimenting or Grooming?

If your kids are older, discuss the NSES's presumption that they can learn about their sexual identity by experimenting with all the options. In the main book's afterword, maxim 15 (page 308) reminds us that people can train their brains what to crave. If this is true, how might experimenting with sexuality outside God's design actually lead them to *prefer* an unbiblical sexuality?

8. On page 99, we are introduced to queer theory and its claims about language. According to this theory, words are not just information. They are also a means of ________________________________

____

____

9. Queer theorists believe words are social constructs used by the oppressor class to marginalize minority groups. Queer theorists also believe that gender is a social construct independent of biology, and "if society made the two-gender rule, they can make the 72-gender rule" (page 100).

   According to this theory, how are words being used as a form of oppression?

10. As a worldview, Marxism rarely shows up the same way twice, cropping up in new and inventive ways and trying to infect us with unbiblical beliefs. Constant through the changes in appearance, however, are (1) the dividing of people into groups and then pitting them against one another and, (2) the progressive push toward freedom from sexual repression and oppression. While many of us are seeing the ugly fruit of these ideas influencing our children in new and alarming ways, the seeds were planted long ago. In the space below, summarize the three main assumptions of a Marxist worldview from pages 101–102:

Assumption 1: ________________________________

____

Assumption 2: ________________________________

____

Assumption 3: ________________________________

____

11. Marxism answers many of the same questions the Christian worldview answers, albeit very differently. Refer to page 103 to complete the chart:

QUESTION	MARXISM'S ANSWER	CHRISTIANITY'S ANSWER
Why are we here?		

What is morality?		
What is wrong with the world?		
How are we redeemed from what is wrong with the world?		

12. Reflect on the differences between the answers. How have you seen the Marxist worldview at work in our culture?

13. Look at the "Matrix of Domination" on page 104.

    a. Define yourself according to this matrix.

b. How does this identity compare to your identity in Christ (Galatians 3:28)?

c. Teaching our kids to defend individuals who are experiencing mistreatment is different from teaching them to defend entire classes of people. Why is this an important distinction (page 105)?

 *Identity in Christ*

Talk to your kids about different jobs and the personality traits and roles that are included with the job description. What are some of the requirements of teachers, and what personal qualities make them effective at their job? How about nurses? Computer programmers? If we were to create a "job description" for Christians, what might that look like? What are some of the roles and requirements of a Christian? (You might mention being salt and light, taking up your cross, loving God and others, and obeying the Lord's commands.) What are some traits we should be committed to embodying? (Hint: Check out Galatians 5:22-23.) How should our everyday decisions flow from being a disciple of Jesus Christ? How can this primary identity inform the way we live in the world?

KEY SCRIPTURES

We encourage you to read the following verses in context (meaning, read at least the entire chapter). Reflect on how they relate to what you're learning, and thank God for the hope and guidance found in His Word.

- Matthew 5:16: "In the same way, let your light shine before others, so that they may see your good works and give glory to your Father who is in heaven."
- Romans 13:1: "Let every person be subject to the governing authorities. For there is no authority except from God, and those that exist have been instituted by God."
- 2 Timothy 4:3-4: "The time is coming when people will not endure sound teaching, but having itching ears they will accumulate for themselves teachers to suit their own passions, and will turn away from listening to the truth and wander off into myths."

PAWS FOR PRAYER

In closing this chapter, reflect on what you learned in lesson 5 and journal your prayer to God here:

Praise:

Admit:

Worship with thanksgiving:

Supplication (submit your requests):

LESSON 6

The Enemy's New Playbook

The Language and Morality of the Sexual Agenda

The agenda (yes, agenda!) to erase biblical sexuality is not new; nor is it an organic, grassroots movement. It is extensively funded and has been strategically planned and executed.[1] And very successfully, I might add.

We trip and fall when we can't see what's in front of us. The enemy loves for us to operate in the dark, but no more, Mama Bears! It's time to shine a big ol' spotlight on his schemes. And remember, when we say the "enemy," we mean *the* enemy—Satan and his demons who have captivated people through hollow and deceptive philosophies, and not the people he has captured (2 Timothy 2:24-26).

The first two tactics—moralization and repetition—are prevalent for everything in this book. Next, we will discuss the importance of words and how our culture has hijacked language, tricking our Christian kids into affirming unbiblical principles using biblical words, concepts, and virtues. These tactics are all being used to establish a new moral code and erode our kids' ability to understand and live out God's design for sexuality.

—*Mama Bear Apologetics Guide to Sexuality and Gender Identity*, pages 111–112

ACTIVE READING NOTES

READING FOCUS	MY RESPONSE
BEFORE YOU READ:	
After skimming the chapter title and subheads, what is one question you would like to have answered in the chapter?	My question:
WHILE YOU READ:	
List three words you discovered in the chapter in addition to the words we have provided.	My words: Book words: *semantic shift* (page 115)— *linguistic theft* (page 115)— *categorical words* (page 116)— *linguistic smuggling* (page 116)—

AFTER YOU READ:	
Did you find an answer to your pre-reading question? (We hope so.) If yes, write it down.	My answer:
List three things you highlighted or underlined in the chapter. This can be new information you learned, encouraging reinforcements of things you already knew, or just plain anything that popped out at you.	My "Aha!" moments: 1. 2. 3.

PICK A QUESTION

Use this space to review the study questions at the end of the chapter and respond to the one you find most thought-provoking or convicting.

EMPOWERING WORDS

- *Denotation*—The dictionary definition or primary meaning of a word, as opposed to the feelings or ideas the word suggests.

- *Connotation*—The positive or negative feelings evoked from a word in addition to its literal or primary meaning.
- *Category error* (or *mistake)*—The error made when a property is incorrectly ascribed to a thing that could not possibly have that property. For example, "The number two is blue."

EMPOWERING THOUGHTS

One popular postmodern approach to words is to declare that words are meaningless. They're just made-up, useful fictions, and we can't really pin them down to any singular meaning. True, there are different words in different languages that may mean the same thing, so in that sense, words are "made-up." But words are very powerful because they *refer to real things.* Words are how we interact with reality. Words are so important that in John 1:1, Jesus Himself is referred to as "the Word." So if your kids come to you with this line of argument (as one of our Mama Bear's children recently did), help them clarify their thoughts: "So, I hear you *using words* to describe how words are meaningless. Is that right?" Then use their own "logic" to reinforce how important words are in the real world. You might say, "What I just heard you say was that you are going to come home after school and clean the whole kitchen, do the dishes, and wash the dog. If words are made-up, then I'm free to interpret your words any way I want, right? Thanks!"

All this goes to show that when you deviate from a Christian worldview, chaos is not far behind. Properly understood and applied, the biblical worldview is the foundation of an orderly and coherent world. Just for fun, brainstorm what you think would happen to our world if everyone woke up and decided that words were meaningless. What parts of society would crumble or cease to function?

Category or Information?

Look at the following categorical statements with your children. Beneath each, write a scenario that would provide actual information that would make the statement true. For example, in the first space, I (Hillary) might say, "The teacher yells at me for things other kids do and even yelled at me on a day I was absent." (#truestory) That might make the statement "My teacher hates me" true. (And she did. I still don't know why.) But, what if your child said, "My teacher always gives me a bad grade." Does this mean the teacher hates them? Not necessarily, and especially not if we are talking about math. Specific statements give you an opportunity to correct your children's categories and asking them for more information helps them better articulate objective statements.

STATEMENT	HYPOTHETICAL ACTION THAT WOULD MAKE THE STATEMENT *TRUE*
My teacher hates me!	
Aidan is such a bully.	
You're always so selfish.	
I can't trust Allison.	

Please note: If a person or a situation is making your child uncomfortable, he or she might not be able to articulate why. Sometimes it's best to listen to our gut. That's perfectly fine! But this exercise can help children build the muscle of articulating their perceptions and conclusions.

1. Read the last paragraph under the heading "Categories Versus Actual Information" on page 117. Explain what can happen to children who have been raised to respect authority when words are smuggled into incorrect categories.

2. The straw man fallacy is a logical error in which someone creates a parody of their opponent's position, exaggerating it in such a way that no reasonable person would agree with it. This makes it easier to refute. We see this happen with hot-button topics like abortion. Have you seen the pro-life and pro-choice positions mischaracterize each other's position? Give examples of their "straw man" version of the other.

3. Where else have you seen "straw man" arguments constructed?

4. Do you think the church is innocent of this? Why or why not?

DIGGING DEEPER

1. In your own words, explain the tactic of moralizing evil (pages 112–113).

2. Can you give an example of moralizing evil from a popular movie? How does this tactic put a positive spin on an action or attitude that would not normally be condoned by Christians?

3. Repetition in and of itself is not good or bad (page 113).
   - List two positive outcomes of repetition from your own life:

   - List two negative outcomes of repetition from your own life:

4. After reading pages 115–116, explain the war on words. What is needed to have a true identity, and why does messing with the identity of humans and God have an impact on our ability to communicate the gospel?

The Power of Positive Repetition

Consider an area in which your child is struggling. What is a *truthful* statement that you can speak over him to encourage him? (Be careful not to tell him he's great at something if he's not.) Repeat your encouragement every day—even multiple times a day if it feels natural. Do this for at least a week. Do you see any difference in your child's attitude regarding their struggle? What does this show us about the importance of positive repetition?

5. Linguistic theft and smuggling are effective tactics of the enemy for a variety of reasons. List four reasons given in the chapter (pages 117–119):

   - ____________________________________
   - ____________________________________
   - ____________________________________
   - ____________________________________

6. Describe a time when you or your children witnessed one of the consequences of the enemy's tactics listed above:

7. Fill in the blanks from the section on stolen words (pages 119–123):

   - *Diversity*: When they say diversity, they do not mean diversity of __________ or ________. They mean diversity of _______________. They want people who all look different but who basically ___________________ the same thing.
   - *Inclusion*: Inclusion means getting rid of the idea of ____________, because if someone doesn't *feel* like they are seen as "_________," then they are (by fiat) being _______________.
   - *Harm*: We must remind our children that something can _________________ without ____________________________.

- *Injustice*: Our world treats ________________________ as synonymous with ______________________________.
  If anything is _______________, then it is ___________.
- *Marriage*: While different forms of marriage are__________ in Scripture (usually multiple wives), that is not God's ____________________________ of marriage.
- *Health/Healthcare*: We cannot define what is ________________ unless we understand how we as humans were intended to _____________—which assumes ___________...which suggests a _______________...which implies an _____________________.
- *Power, Authority, and Oppression*: Just because _______ authorities exist doesn't mean that _____________ itself is bad.

KEY SCRIPTURES

We encourage you to read the following verses in context (read at least the entire chapter), reflect on how they relate to what you're learning, and thank God for the hope and guidance found in His Word.

- Deuteronomy 32:4: "The Rock, his work is perfect, for all his ways are justice. A God of faithfulness and without iniquity, just and upright is he."
- Romans 12:21: "Do not be overcome by evil, but overcome evil with good."
- 3 John 11: "Beloved, do not imitate evil but imitate good. Whoever does good is from God; whoever does evil has not seen God."
- Exodus 32:5: "Aaron...built an altar before [the calf]. And Aaron made a proclamation and said, 'Tomorrow shall be a feast to the LORD.'"
- 1 John 3:18: "Little children, let us not love in word or talk but in deed and in truth."

PAWS FOR PRAYER

In closing this chapter, reflect on what you learned in lesson 6 and journal your prayer to God here:

Praise:

Admit:

Worship with thanksgiving:

Supplication (submit your requests):

LESSON 7

The Genderbread Person

The New Definitions of Identity, Expression, Sex, and Attraction

Friends, we were created by God for relationship, and healthy relationships include an emotional component. What has happened to our understanding of healthy, platonic, same-sex friendship? If our kids are buying into the propaganda that a desire for an emotional attachment with someone of the same sex means they have a same-sex sexual orientation, then be prepared for a lot of confusion. Healthy relationships begin with healthy same-sex friendships.[1] We cannot take a normal desire and make it a predictor of sexual identity. By this definition, everyone is romantically attracted to their best friends.

—*Mama Bear Apologetics Guide to Sexuality and Gender Identity*, page 137

ACTIVE READING NOTES

READING FOCUS	MY RESPONSE
BEFORE YOU READ:	
After skimming the chapter title and subheads, what is one question you would like to have answered in the chapter?	My question:
WHILE YOU READ:	
List three words you discovered in the chapter in addition to the words we have provided.	My words: Book words: *law of identity* (page 128)—
AFTER YOU READ:	
Did you find an answer to your pre-reading question? (We hope so.) If yes, write it down.	My answer:
List three things you highlighted or underlined in the chapter. This can be new information you learned, encouraging reinforcements of things you already knew, or just plain anything that popped out at you.	My "Aha!" moments: 1. 2. 3.

PICK A QUESTION

Use this space to review the study questions at the end of the chapter and respond to the one you find most thought-provoking or convicting.

EMPOWERING WORDS

- *Pedagogy*—The study of teaching methods, instructional approaches, and theories informing how students learn.
- *Law of non-contradiction*—A foundational principle of logic stating that contradictory propositions cannot both be true in the same sense at the same time. For example, an animal cannot be a dog and not a dog at the same time in the same sense.
- *False dichotomy*—When two options are falsely presented as the only two options. For example, "You either accept my identity or you don't love me."

EMPOWERING THOUGHTS

While the English language has just one word for *love*, biblical Greek has four words to describe the different kinds of affection people can experience for one another—*agape, eros, phileo,* and *storge.*

Storge: Family love—the natural and mutual affection between family members.

Phileo: Friendship—an emotional connection going deeper than casual acquaintance.

Eros: Romantic love—feelings of sexual attraction and desire.

Agape: Spiritual love—self-sacrificial love that does not require any particular emotion.

Distinguishing Loves

Regularly talk with your children about the different kinds of love. Be on the lookout for expressions of these loves in culture and in community. When you see friends laughing together (*phileo*), nurses caring for their patients (*agape*), a couple kissing (*eros*), or a family enjoying time together (*storge*), ask your children to identify the type of love they see expressed. Don't be shy about putting the TV on pause and asking this question as y'all watch together. Like the maxims in the main book's afterword, this exercise should be done until your kids want to gag—no, seriously...*until they want to gag*—because our culture is telling your kids that *all* their feelings of attraction are erotic. The more familiar your children are with the different types of love, the less vulnerable they will be to mistaking their own feelings of friendship for those of romance.

DIGGING DEEPER

1. In the book, we learn about the Genderbread Person. Draw your own Genderbread Person below and label identity, attraction, expression, and sex.

2. Before reading this book, were you aware of curricula like the Genderbread Person (or Gender Unicorn)? Do you know if these tools are being used in local schools around you?

3. Our lack of awareness has no bearing on something's existence. On page 128, we learn that the Genderbread curriculum is teaching the opposite. Rather than teaching that identity is objectively verifiable (outside of us), students are learning that gender identity is dependent on self-perception (thoughts and feelings). This removes gender from the realm of objective reality and into the realm of subjective preference or experience. If our children learn that their gender identity is based upon feelings (subjective), what other things might they believe to be true about themselves?

4. On page 129, we read, "If our kids think their identity is based on how they identify in the moment, then there is no security in Christ. If they don't *feel* saved, then they aren't. If they don't *feel* like God is close to them at the moment, then He's not. If they *feel* ugly, then they are. Don't try to talk them out of it: The Genderbread Person taught them all about how to determine their identity." What are the consequences of affirming the above examples?

What Makes Me...Me

Ask your children to describe themselves. How do they do it? Is it by their hobbies? Their gender? Their personality traits? Their strengths or weaknesses? Their academic pursuits? What parts of their self-identification can change? What parts will never change?

5. On the next page, summarize in one or two sentences the Genderbread Person's main interpretations of the following elements:

Identity (pages 128–131):

Expression (pages 121–133):

Sex (pages 133–136):

Attraction (pages 136–138):

6. Read pages 129–131. What are gender stereotypes? In what ways can they be helpful if applied loosely? In what ways can they be damaging if applied too rigidly?

7. Do you think the transgender movement builds up gender stereotypes or breaks them down? Why?

8. What problems do you foresee with defining sexualities if the concept of biological gender has been erased?

9. What sexual and gender identities have you heard discussed (for example, *nonbinary* or *gender fluid*)?

10. Fill in the blanks (pages 138–140):

   a. We were created by a _______ God for _________, and our families, friendships, and communities give us a picture of the way God relates to us.

   b. We are by nature ____________ to ____________ things, but ___________ for beauty does not equal ____________ attraction.

   c. We need to reaffirm to our kids what kinds of touch are ________________ and ______________.

   d. Together, we _______ the *imago dei* in a way that ________ and ________ cannot on their own.

KEY SCRIPTURES

We encourage you to read the following verses in context (meaning, read at least the entire chapter). Reflect on how they relate to what you're learning, and thank God for the hope and guidance found in His Word.

- Matthew 7:24: "Everyone then who hears these words of mine and does them will be like a wise man who built his house on the rock."
- Hebrews 13:8: "Jesus Christ is the same yesterday and today and forever."
- Deuteronomy 11:19: "You shall teach [these words] to your children, talking of them when you are sitting in your house, and when you are walking by the way, and when you lie down, and when you rise."

PAWS FOR PRAYER

In closing this chapter, reflect on what you learned in lesson 7 and journal your prayer to God here:

Praise:

Admit:

Worship with thanksgiving:

Supplication (submit your requests):

LESSON 8

Sex-Positivity

Anything Goes If It's Consensual

The more value something has, the more rules and boundaries we erect to protect it...Only when something doesn't have any inherent value can you do whatever you want with it, which turns out to be the skeleton lurking in the closet of sex-positivity. It encourages you to do whatever you want with whomever you want. The implicit message (that most people don't pick up on) is that you and your partner(s) have no inherent value worth protecting. Consent can't provide this value, and neither can pleasure. Sure, sex-positivity may sound like freedom, but in reality, it's saying that your body and what you do with it don't matter.

—*Mama Bear Apologetics Guide to Sexuality and Gender Identity*, page 150

ACTIVE READING NOTES

READING FOCUS	MY RESPONSE
BEFORE YOU READ:	
After skimming the chapter title and subheads, what is one question you would like to have answered in the chapter?	My question:
WHILE YOU READ:	
List three words you discovered in the chapter in addition to the words we have provided.	My words: Book words: *death* (page 148)— *moral relativism* (page 148)— *inherent value* (page 149)—
AFTER YOU READ:	
Did you find an answer to your pre-reading question? (We hope so.) If yes, write it down.	My answer:

List three things you highlighted or underlined in the chapter. This can be new information you learned, encouraging reinforcements of things you already knew, or just plain anything that popped out at you.	My "Aha!" moments: 1. 2. 3.

PICK A QUESTION

Use this space to review the study questions at the end of the chapter and respond to the one you find most thought-provoking or convicting.

EMPOWERING WORDS

- *Traditionalist view*—Scripture teaches that sexual activity was designed for and intended to be enjoyed between a husband and wife.
- *Revisionist view*—Since loving, consensual, monogamous, same-sex relations are not explicitly prohibited in Scripture, they can be blessed by God—even holy—and should be included in the life of the church.
- *Taboos*—Cultural prohibitions on behaviors deemed unnatural, unhealthy, or otherwise unacceptable.

- *Desensitization*—The process of exposing a person to a stimulus (an idea, a picture, etc.) so many times the stimulus is eventually seen as normal and no longer provokes an emotional response.

Illustrating Desensitization

Ask your children if they have ever tried to approach an animal—a dog, a cat, or a bird—and had it run away from them. What about approaching a pet that knew them? From the perspective of the animal, why does one flee and the other respond happily? Talk with your children about how *familiarity breeds feelings of safety* and discuss how this also applies to our instinctual reactions to unbiblical worldviews. The more we are exposed to anti-biblical views, the safer (and more normal) they seem. Sex-positivity relies on the process of desensitization.

EMPOWERING THOUGHTS

1. Culture tells our teens that social media presence leads to validation, and sexual promiscuity is a positive way to get to know yourself. According to the Christian worldview, how do we:

    a. Achieve validation? (See Romans 14:17-19; 2 Corinthians 10:18; Colossians 3:23-24)

    b. Get to know ourselves in a positive way? (See Romans 12:3-8.)

2. In 1 Corinthians 6:12, the apostle Paul explains, "'All things are lawful for me,' but not all things are helpful. 'All things are lawful for me,' but I will not be dominated by anything." How is the Christian view—that not every sexual act is beneficial—at odds with sex-positivity's claim that any consensual and pleasurable act is good?

3. What is the source of morality according to Scripture? Is it an objective or subjective source? Explain. (Hint: See pages 47–49 in chapter 2.)

4. Scripture talks about two different types of judgment—one of which is biblically condemned (Matthew 7:1-5; Luke 6:37-42; Romans 2:1-3) and one of which is biblically commanded (Leviticus 19:15; John 7:24; 1 Corinthians 5:11-13). What are the differences between these two types of judgment?

5. In light of those passages, how would you respond to a person who claims that the Bible says not to judge?

DIGGING DEEPER

1. Chapter 8 opens with a brief look at the origins of the sexual revolution of the '60s, especially the influence of Wilhelm Reich. To answer the questions below, see pages 143–144.

   a. What was Reich's goal?

   b. What did he encourage?

   c. What did he champion?

   d. What did he assert led to health and even salvation?

2. As God's image bearers, we are created with a divinely designed purpose that includes a compulsion to worship. Of course, we are to worship God who alone does all things motivated by pure love, goodness, and understanding of what leads to human flourishing. Reich's materialistic view of the universe does not allow for the existence of a supernatural God, but even he demonstrates this God-given compulsion to worship.

a. What do your answers above reveal about the object of Reich's worship?

b. What do you think it means to worship?

c. Where have you been tempted to direct your worship?

It's Time to ROAR Like a Mother at Sex-Positivity

Recognize the Message

3. Summarize sex-positivity in your own words.

4. Consider the three key points of sex-positivity. Which have you encountered most often and where? (See pages 145–146.)

5. Sometimes cultural taboos are evidence of God's law written on our hearts. How might you discern the difference between your own preferences and evidence of God's design?

6. How do you think a sex-positive person would evaluate a sexual act that was physically harmful, but to which a person had consented and claimed to enjoy? In what ways can sex-positivity be at odds with promoting health and well-being?

Offer Discernment

7. Identify and explain what we can learn from sex-positivity. What truths does it offer, or what motives can we dignify? (See pages 146–147.)

8. Identify and explain the seven main lies of sex-positivity (pages 147–152). Highlight or underline the three that, in your opinion, most greatly undermine the biblical sexual ethic. If you're with a group, share which three lies you selected and discuss why. For each lie, provide an example of a biblical truth that is twisted by sex-positivity.

LIE	EXPLANATION	WHAT BIBLICAL TRUTH IS TWISTED BY THIS LIE?
If it's consensual, it's moral.		
Pleasure is the only purpose of sex.		
All judgments (except this one!) are wrong!		
Sex-positivity leads to freedom.		
All expressions of sexuality are healthy.		
You can be a sex-positive Christian.		
If you're not for us, you're sex-negative!		

Argue for a Healthier Approach

9. Consider the three truths listed on pages 152–153. Which do you think is most challenging for kids to understand, and why?

Reinforce with Discussion, Discipleship, and Prayer

10. Give your own examples of how children can be taught to understand the consequences of having no rules.

11. How can we explain to our kids the difference between using good judgment and being judgmental? (Hint: Matthew 7:1-5; John 7:24; Romans 14:4; 1 Peter 4:17)

KEY SCRIPTURES

We encourage you to read the following verses in context (meaning, read at least the entire chapter). Reflect on how they relate to what you're learning, and thank God for the hope and guidance found in His Word.

- Ephesians 4:30: "Do not grieve the Holy Spirit of God, by whom you were sealed for the day of redemption."
- Psalm 25:9: "He leads the humble in what is right, and teaches the humble his way."
- Galatians 5:1: "For freedom Christ has set us free; stand firm therefore, and do not submit again to a yoke of slavery."
- Romans 1:25: "They exchanged the truth about God for a lie and worshiped and served the creature rather than the Creator, who is blessed forever!"

PAWS FOR PRAYER

In closing this chapter, reflect on what you learned in lesson 8 and journal your prayer to God here:

Praise:

Admit:

Worship with thanksgiving:

Supplication (submit your requests):

LESSON 9

Queer Theory

A Whole New World(view)

Christianity is being pitted against a worldview [queer theory] that answers [worldview] questions very differently—especially the questions regarding morality...The confusing thing about queer theory is that it isn't (what I'd call) a *positive* theory, meaning that it aims *at* something... [Queer theory] is defined primarily by what it stands *against*. And what does it stand against? Anything that is considered *normal*...You'll hear the phrase "authentic self" tossed around a lot. Queer theory teaches that the authentic self is who (or what) the person *would* have been (or how they would have identified) had they not been constrained by society's norms...According to queer theory, people "not following the norm" in their dress or behavior is them *being true to their identity*. For example, a person doesn't just enjoy dressing like an animal (furry), but they identify *as* an animal (therian).[1] A person doesn't just wear a fairy or elf costume (cosplay); they now identify *as* a fairy or an elf (otherkin).[2] Forget male and female; what it means to be *human* is now up for debate.

—*Mama Bear Apologetics Guide to Sexuality and Gender Identity*, pages 160, 163, 165, and 164

ACTIVE READING NOTES

READING FOCUS	MY RESPONSE
BEFORE YOU READ:	
After skimming the chapter title and subheads, what is one question you would like to have answered in the chapter?	My question:
WHILE YOU READ:	
List three words you discovered in the chapter in addition to the words we have provided.	My words: Book words: *social power* (page 162)— *cultural norms* (page 162)— *queer theory* (page 164)— *furry* (page 164)— *therian* (page 164)— *cosplay* (page 164)—

	otherkin (page 164)—
	social construct (page 166)—

AFTER YOU READ:

Did you find an answer to your pre-reading question? (We hope so.) If yes, write it down.	My answer:
List three things you highlighted or underlined in the chapter. This can be new information you learned, encouraging reinforcements of things you already knew, or just plain anything that popped out at you.	My "Aha!" moments: 1. 2. 3.

PICK A QUESTION

Use this space to review the study questions at the end of the chapter and respond to the one you find most thought-provoking or convicting.

EMPOWERING WORDS

- *Critical theory (CT)*—A cluster of social theories that attempt to explain how the world operates by defining who does and does not have power to shape society. CT also proposes how society should operate by promoting social activism as a tool to redistribute said power among social groups.
- *Binary*—A system that gives only two options and nothing in between. If someone identifies as *non*binary, they believe they are breaking away from the binary of manhood and womanhood and opting for a third option.
- *Authentic self*—According to queer theory, the authentic self is who (or what) someone would have been (or how they would have identified) had they not been constrained by society's norms.
- *Norms*—Socially and culturally accepted behaviors, identities, and ways of presenting. In queer theory, norms are generally seen as oppressive barriers to be broken down.
- *Morality*—How right and wrong are generally defined. According to queer theory, morality is allowing people to accurately identify as their true self and live freely as that self without stigma or social constraints.
- *All-or-nothing thinking*—A cognitive distortion (also called black-and-white thinking) where things are all one way or

another. A person engaging in all-or-nothing thinking will provide as many examples for their case as possible, as if doing so can prove that *all* things are as they describe.

- *Stigma*—A negative attitude toward a person, trait, or behavior that is deemed socially unacceptable by the majority, leading people to avoid the person who has the trait or behavior.

EMPOWERING THOUGHTS

For a look at how the Bible defines sexual norms, read the list of forbidden sexual relationships given in Leviticus 18. Here we see commandments such as, "No one is to approach any close relative to have sexual relations" (verse 6 NIV), "Do not have sexual relations with your neighbor's wife" (verse 20 NIV), and "Do not have sexual relations with an animal" (verse 23 NIV). We also find the Bible's first explicit commandment against homosexuality (verse 22). Until relatively recently, we've largely seen these commands reflected in the sexual norms that most cultures have held as acceptable—and while sexual sin has been something humans have wrestled with since the fall, having these standards for sexuality has been a net positive for humankind.

1. As you read Leviticus 18, what is your reaction? Do any commands surprise you—either because you didn't know they were wrong or because you can't believe they had to be included in the list? What does the fact that God knew He had to provide such clear instruction in this area say about humankind?

2. How would you respond to someone who said social sexual norms are the *cause* of harm and oppression? How might they be defining harm?

3. How do God's clear commands of what Christians should and should not do challenge queer theory's notion of the authentic self? In your own life, have you ever felt that any of the Bible's commands (not just the ones regarding sex) were holding you back from expressing yourself? Which ones? How do you feel they have held you back? Pray and ask God if you are believing any lies about yourself or what Scripture says.

DIGGING DEEPER

1. If a person believes the lie that "claiming to know truth is a power play," what does that do to the concept of the Bible being true? What about the gospel being true? What about Jesus as the way, the *truth*, and the life? What else crumbles under the lie that all truths are ultimately power plays?

2. What does it mean on page 163 that queer theory isn't a "positive" theory? How is queer theory defined?

3. Consider how queer theory responds to the five major worldview tenets on pages 165–169.

WORLDVIEW QUESTION	HOW QUEER THEORY ANSWERS OR DEFINES	IMPLICATIONS FOR SEXUALITY
Human origin and identity		
Truth and reality		
Brokenness		
Morality		
Redemption		

4. Have you encountered any of these facets of queer theory in your own life? Have you seen these beliefs leading people astray? Have you noticed any of the tenets of queer theory creeping into the church? Describe or discuss.

5. Fill in the blanks from this quote on page 172: ________ and ________ do not change our *identity* in Christ, and the end goal of our identity is ____________, not ______________.

   What makes this statement so countercultural?

6. Consider one social norm you fall outside of that has led you to feel as though you don't fit in. How has this impacted your life? How can you use this experience to have compassion for those who struggle with feeling they fall outside of sexual or gender norms?

7. Read through the four main messages in the ROAR section (pages 170–171). Which of these four have you heard the most? Which two of the four have you been most tempted to believe and why did you choose those two?

8. Read the offering discernment section on pages 171–172. Fill in the following blanks and answer the question:

   Words can create __________________________ to help us better ________________ the world and each other...But people misuse language when they take a ____________________ and turn it into an _________________________, an immutable "I am" statement that is outside their control.

   What do you think is the main difference between these two uses of words?

9. Three out of the four lies on pages 172–173 involve all-or-nothing thinking. How would you converse with a person to help them realize that their conclusions are based on all-or-nothing thinking? How can the ROAR method help you interact with people who are prone to all-or-nothing thinking?

10. Some norms and stigmas exist for good reason. List three gender or sexual norms for each of the following:

    Good/Healthy/Biblical Norms:

Unfair Socially Constructed and Extrabiblical Norms:

KEY SCRIPTURES

We encourage you to read the following verses in context (meaning, read at least the entire chapter). Reflect on how they relate to what you're learning, and thank God for the hope and guidance found in His Word.

- 1 John 3:19-20: "This is how we know that we belong to the truth and how we set our hearts at rest in his presence: If our hearts condemn us, we know that God is greater than our hearts, and he knows everything" (NIV).
- Psalm 119:160: "All your words are true; all your righteous laws are eternal" (NIV).
- Psalm 16:8, 11: "I keep my eyes always on the LORD. With him at my right hand, I will not be shaken...You make known to me the path of life; you will fill me with joy in your presence, with eternal pleasures at your right hand."
- Luke 9:23: "Whoever wants to be my disciple must deny themselves and take up their cross daily and follow me" (NIV).
- Proverbs 3:5, 7: "Trust in the LORD with all your heart and lean not on your own understanding...Do not be wise in your own eyes; fear the LORD and shun evil" (NIV).

PAWS FOR PRAYER

In closing this chapter, reflect on what you learned in lesson 9 and journal your prayer to God here:

Praise:

Admit:

Worship with thanksgiving:

Supplication (submit your requests):

PART 3

Things That Are Tripping Everyone Up

In part 1, we learned what God wants to communicate through human sexuality. We learned about the power of sex and how destructive it is when misused. We also defined and explained the beauty of a biblical worldview, including how it affects the way we view sexuality. In part 2, we learned about an unbiblical worldview that is shaping and influencing public education and secular thought today.

As we turn the last corner into part 3, we will take a closer look at how these false teachings sneak into our lives, the lives of our kids, and even the lives of our churches—justifying their presence under the new "biblical" interpretations of love and inclusivity. We will look at each issue, identify where the church has compromised and fallen short, and set our sights on how we can love people better—the way the Bible says. The gospel is our greatest hope; we are all equal at the foot of the cross, equally fallen and equally offered redemption.

LESSON 10

Purity Culture

When Our Best Efforts Went Kablooey

The purity movement was not an unmitigated success, too often inadvertently sending the message that sexual sin was the one sin God couldn't forgive...Overly zealous church leaders made virginity their primary focus, neglecting the redemptive work of Christ. Some even ignored the original design of their curriculum by excluding parents, refusing to be transparent about what was being taught, or by integrating their own perverted twists to the lessons[1]...[Some people] were so browbeaten into shame that they would rather toss any semblance of morality than return to being compared to chewed-up bubble gum...We don't abandon truth because of its abuses. We correct the abuses and stand firm in the truth.

—*Mama Bear Apologetics Guide to Sexuality and Gender Identity*, pages 181, 182, and 185

ACTIVE READING NOTES

READING FOCUS	MY RESPONSE
BEFORE YOU READ:	
After skimming the chapter title and subheads, what is one question you would like to have answered in the chapter?	My question:
WHILE YOU READ:	
List three words you discovered in the chapter in addition to the words we have provided.	My words: Book words: *chastity* (page 189)— *sexual integrity* (page 194)—
AFTER YOU READ:	
Did you find an answer to your pre-reading question? (We hope so.) If yes, write it down.	My answer:

List three things you highlighted or underlined in the chapter. This can be new information you learned, encouraging reinforcements of things you already knew, or just plain anything that popped out at you.	My "Aha!" moments: 1. 2. 3.

PICK A QUESTION

Use this space to review the study questions at the end of the chapter and respond to the one you find most thought-provoking or convicting.

EMPOWERING WORDS

- *Covenant*—An agreement between two parties that establishes their relational identity to one another as well as their roles within the relationship. It is usually enacted by having (1) a formal agreement and (2) a sign of the covenant.
- *Inherited guilt*—Biblical doctrine that says we are all counted guilty because God has righteously imputed Adam's guilt to all of us (Romans 5:12-21).
- *Inherited corruption*—Biblical doctrine that teaches we are all

born having inherited a sinful nature through Adam (Psalm 51:1-5).

- *Regeneration*—A supernatural act of God that re-establishes the spiritual life inside us that died and was lost in the garden (John 3:3-8).

EMPOWERING THOUGHTS

Many people read the original sexual purity curriculum and find very little if anything they disagree with. In its infancy, purity curricula set out to engage both youth groups and parents in the meaningful role of lovingly and intentionally discipling children in biblical sexuality. Over time, the messaging became distorted—even abusive. Rather than holiness and freedom, the fruit was often shame and fear.

1. Why do you think good teachings often get distorted beyond recognition?

2. How did purity culture eventually distort or even contradict the doctrine of salvation by grace through faith?

3. Did your church or school use any purity culture curricula? Was your experience positive or negative? How did the teaching either (1) help you understand the truth of the gospel more clearly or (2) distort the gospel message?

4. Our sexuality and sexual ethic develop over time and are influenced by multiple players: parents, church, school, culture (especially social media), life experience, and peers.

   a. Which of these influences played the most significant role in the development of your own sexuality and sexual ethic?

   b. If you could talk to your teenage self, which misconception would you like to correct?

   c. How might you encourage parents who minimize their role or who believe they are too late to influence their children's beliefs about sexuality?

Purity Versus Protection

Purity culture tends to emphasize purity (duh). But remember the discussion from lessons 1, 2, and 3. Sexual faithfulness isn't just about purity; it is about understanding *the God who is* while safeguarding ourselves from a force so powerful it requires protection and boundaries.

Ask your kids what they do to protect themselves from the sun. They might mention sunglasses, sunscreen, hats, etc. Remind them that God's commands regarding sexuality are put in place for their protection. How is protecting oneself a purer motive than guarding our reputations?

DIGGING DEEPER

1. Complete the following paragraph by filling in the blanks from page 182:

   Our kids deserve the truth—that God's plan for sex starts with marriage—but when the truth has been abused and twisted by the people we trust most, it no longer looks attractive…and can seem downright terrifying. We don't abandon ____________________ because of its __________________. We ____________ the abuses and stand firm in the ____________.

2. Which biblical truths did the original purity curricula emphasize?

3. What were some unintended consequences of the purity message gone wrong?

4. Have you experienced any of the unintended baggage brought about by purity culture in your own life? If so, share or reflect briefly.

5. What are some ways in which the missteps or lies of purity culture might have affected girls differently than boys?

It's Time to ROAR Like a Mother at Purity Culture

Recognize the Message

6. Fill out the chart by doing the following:

   a. Identify three of the main messages of purity culture found on pages 186–189.

   b. In your own words, explain what is damaging about each of the three purity culture missteps.

   c. Now correct each distortion with a statement that is theologically true and directly refutes the message and the damage.

THE MESSAGE	THE DAMAGE	HEALTHY TRUTH STATEMENT

THE MESSAGE	THE DAMAGE	HEALTHY TRUTH STATEMENT

7. Purity culture told girls their bodies could be stumbling blocks over which boys might trip. Stumbling blocks are objects. Though opposite to the desired goal, can you think of ways in which pornography and purity culture might lead to similar ends?

Offer Discernment

8. What important distinction related to holiness and chastity was missing from much of the purity movement? (See page 189.)

9. Many students mistakenly thought their physical virginity was essential for __________________________. (See page 189.)

10. How do our clothing choices actually communicate something about us?

11. Consider the three lies of purity culture (pages 190–192). Which could bring the most baggage into a good marriage?

Argue for a Healthier Approach

12. Redemption is possible for ________________. No amount of sexual brokenness can keep you from the ____________ power of God (page 192).

13. Define *chastity* and share in your own words what we want our kids to understand about it (pages 189–192).

14. What is the best guiding principle for choosing the clothes we will wear? (See pages 192–194.)

Reinforce with Discussion, Discipleship, and Prayer

Modesty has gotten a bad rap. When most Christians refer to dressing "modestly," they usually think of clothing that is less sexy and doesn't show a lot of skin. But that's a more modern understanding, and not exactly how the word *modest* is used in Scripture. Consider the following passage from the *Strong's Lexicon* regarding modesty:

> The Greek adjective κόσμιος (*kosmios*) conveys the idea of being orderly, respectable, or well-behaved. It is used to describe someone who conducts themselves in a manner that is fitting and appropriate, reflecting a sense of decorum and propriety. In the New Testament, it is often associated with the behavior expected of church leaders and believers, emphasizing the importance of living a life that is in harmony with Christian values and teachings. In the Greco-Roman world, the concept of "kosmios" was highly valued, as it was associated with the ideal of living in harmony with the order of the universe. This idea was reflected in social conduct, where individuals were expected to behave in a manner that was fitting and proper within their community. For early Christians, adopting a "kosmios" lifestyle was a way to distinguish themselves from the surrounding pagan culture and to bear witness to the transformative power of the Gospel.[2]

15. How might this change our idea of what it means to be or dress or behave modestly?

16. What are some ways someone could dress in a way that isn't "sexy," but still falls under the purview of "immodest" according to the *Strong's* definition?

KEY SCRIPTURES

We encourage you to read the following verses in context (meaning, read at least the entire chapter). Reflect on how they relate to what you're learning, and thank God for the hope and guidance found in His Word.

- 1 Timothy 2:9: "Women should adorn themselves in respectable apparel, with modesty and self-control, not with braided hair and gold or pearls or costly attire."
- Isaiah 1:18: "Come now, let us reason together, says the LORD: though your sins are like scarlet, they shall be as white as snow; though they are red like crimson, they shall become like wool."
- Isaiah 61:10: "I will greatly rejoice in the LORD; my soul shall exult in my God, for he has clothed me with the garments of salvation; he has covered me with the robe of righteousness, as a bridegroom decks himself like a priest with a beautiful headdress, and as a bride adorns herself with her jewels."
- 1 Corinthians 10:31: "Whether you eat or drink, or whatever you do, do all to the glory of God."
- Matthew 5:8: "Blessed are the pure in heart, for they shall see God."

PAWS FOR PRAYER

In closing this chapter, reflect on what you learned in lesson 10 and journal your prayer to God here:

Praise:

Admit:

Worship with thanksgiving:

Supplication (submit your requests):

LESSON 11

Pornography

It's Not Technically Sex If You're by Yourself, Right?

The younger a child is when they are exposed to suggestive images, the earlier their brains can be wired to seek instant gratification and pleasure. They're also less likely to perceive the dangers and consequences of what they're viewing because the good judgment portion of the brain doesn't fully develop until adulthood. They just see a hot chick, so they'll buy the video game, or watch the movie with the shirtless hunk, and click on the website to see more because it feels good. The adult entertainment industry knows this and is happy to meet their demand. In short: They're using our kids' brains against them, grooming them to be *sensual* consumers instead of sensible ones. How do they get them to be sensual consumers? By hijacking the brain and using its chemicals against them.

—*Mama Bear Apologetics Guide to Sexuality and Gender Identity*, page 202

ACTIVE READING NOTES

READING FOCUS	MY RESPONSE
BEFORE YOU READ:	
After skimming the chapter title and subheads, what is one question you would like to have answered in the chapter?	My question:
WHILE YOU READ:	
List three words you discovered in the chapter in addition to the words we have provided.	My words: Book words: *oxytocin* (page 203)— *vasopressin* (page 203)— *dopamine* (page 204)—
AFTER YOU READ:	
Did you find an answer to your pre-reading question? (We hope so.) If yes, write it down.	My answer:

List three things you highlighted or underlined in the chapter. This can be new information you learned, encouraging reinforcements of things you already knew, or just plain anything that popped out at you.	My "Aha!" moments: 1. 2. 3.

PICK A QUESTION

Use this space to review the study questions at the end of the chapter and respond to the one you find most thought-provoking or convicting.

EMPOWERING WORDS

- *Exploitation*—The act of taking advantage of someone for selfish gain.
- *Addiction*—When a person engages in an action to the point where it is no longer a choice but a compulsion. To achieve feelings of euphoria, they must increasingly escalate the behavior. Due to physiological adaptation, the drive toward the behavior is often no longer motivated on feeling the "high" but rather on merely feeling normal.
- *(Sexual) grooming*—The creation of an interpersonal bond

and sense of safety for the purpose of (sexually) exploiting an individual. Grooming involves intentionally eroding personal boundaries through escalating levels of touch or sexualized content. Often, grooming involves play-acting, discussing, or viewing sexualized material to the point where the intended victim begins to see these behaviors as normal. Once the grooming process is complete, the victimized individual will often *voluntarily* participate in sexual activities they would never have consented to before the grooming process.

- *Pornography*—Any depiction (verbal, auditory, or visual) of erotic or sexually explicit behaviors, usually with the intention (or at least foreknowledge) that consumers will experience sexual arousal.

EMPOWERING THOUGHTS

"Fight the New Drug" (www.FightTheNewDrug.org) is a nonreligious organization united around exposing the devastation to individuals, relationships, and societies caused by pornography. Their website hosts resources including scientific studies, testimonials, and even a documentary series uncovering many of the same troubling trends we discuss in this chapter. We recommend familiarizing yourself with this organization and the work they are doing.

1. How can an organization like this help us demonstrate to our children the validity of the Bible's teachings on human sexuality?

2. How can this organization and its research open up conversations with friends and family who don't come from a Christian background?

DIGGING DEEPER

1. On pages 200–202, we learn some troubling facts about the scope of the pornography problem. Which of the statistics horrified you the most, and why?

2. What makes porn potentially more addictive than other drugs? (See pages 202–204.)

3. "When it comes to pornography, it is not the amount of pornography, but the *type* that changes" (page 205). Explain the significance of this statement.

4. What are the two most commonly used descriptors of pornography? (See page 207.)

   a. Summarize what is meant by *objectification*. (See pages 207–208.)

   b. Summarize what is meant by *dehumanization*. (See pages 208–209.)

It's Time to ROAR Like a Mother at Pornography

Recognize the Message

Consider the three main messages of pornography on pages 209–211. What are the ramifications for a child who believes these lies are true? Can you think of any popular books or movies that promote one of these messages?

MAIN MESSAGE	RAMIFICATIONS	EXAMPLE FROM POP CULTURE

Offer Discernment

5. Unpack this statement: *Sin is often people trying to meet a legitimate need in an illegitimate way.* List some examples that might illustrate this statement.

6. What are some legitimate needs people might be trying to meet with pornography? What might be a better way to meet those needs? (See pages 211–212.)

7. Consider the six main lies of porn as explained on pages 213–215. Which three do you consider to be the *most* enslaving, and why did you choose those three?

    -
    -
    -

Is It Porn If the Characters Are Married?

As Christians, we've taught our kids that sex between a husband and a wife is beautiful. But one of the ways that porn is becoming mainstream is by smuggling in graphic sex scenes between married adults. Ask your older kids if it's okay for us to watch graphic sex if the characters are married. Why or why not?

Furthermore, sex scenes on film and TV are choreographed and manipulated. This leads to confusion for newly married couples who struggle to reconcile sex in the real world with what they saw portrayed in the movies. (As my sister-in-law stated matter-of-factly to me premarriage: "It's not like the movies. Prepare for a lot more...um...noises.")

Skip sex scenes in movies and explain to your kids why! Let your kids know that exploring their sexuality with a spouse will be a lot more fun when they don't have to first *unlearn* the unrealistic portrayals of sex from movies.

Argue for a Healthier Approach

8. Fill in the blanks from page 216: God created the act of sex for ______________ and ______________ to recommit to each other __________ and to connect with one another in a way that transcends ____________ or ____________.

9. Complete these two sentences (page 216):

a. Who (or what) you share your orgasm with matters, *and* ______

____

b. There will likely be some emotional (and physiological) consequences, *and* ________________________________

____

Reinforce with Discussion, Discipleship, and Prayer

Make a list of four healthy experiences that your child (or you) really enjoys (the fun, dopamine-producing things):

-
-
-
-

Are these activities part of your regular routine? If not, what steps can you take as a family to have more healthy fun together?

An Exit Strategy for Porn Exposure

If you want to talk with your son about the dangers of pornography, it'll be key to get his dad or a trusted male mentor involved and equip him with the statistics. Our kids need a way to recuse themselves when their friends are wanting them to look at porn. Many kids aren't even aware it's something they shouldn't look at. Train your children to start out with a soft rejection, such as, "I'm not really into that," or "Can we do something else?"

If they are in a group and the group is still gung ho about looking at porn, encourage your child to just walk away and do something else.

If the situation escalates, they (and especially our sons) will need a game plan for getting out of it without being belittled or emasculated. For the guys, a harder rejection might sound like:

- "Have fun with your fake sex. I'm not quite that desperate."
- "You *do* realize a lot of the women you're watching were trafficked, right?"
- "Are you *trying* to win the record for Youngest Case of Erectile Dysfunction?"

Porn isn't just a boy problem. Anyone can become addicted to it due to the chemicals involved. Our girls need a way to say no too. This is where we need to emphasize the reality of sex trafficking and how it doesn't start in a seedy hotel room. It begins with seeing sexualized images and then wanting to imitate them in order to be popular and accepted. Suggest she use the same tactics as the boys: asking to do something else or walking away. If her friends persist, she can practice saying harder rejection things, such as:

- "Yeah, I'm not into watching women dehumanize themselves."
- "Do you know how many of these videos were coerced? Why do you like watching other girls getting raped?"
- "This makes me sad. I have no idea who this girl is or why she felt like she needed to do this."

Your job as a parent—especially for dads—is to give your girls the attention, healthy touch, and affirmation they so desperately crave.

As your girls get older, they will be tempted to post pictures of themselves on their social media to imitate their favorite celebrities. Ask your girls to pay attention to their images: Are their *face and smile* the main attraction? The company in the photograph or the event they attended? Or is the picture primarily about their bodies, sexy faces, or what they are wearing? If the photo only serves the purpose of telegraphing sexiness—mainly showcasing their bodies or bedroom eyes—talk to them about what it means to objectify themselves and why this is not a route they want to take. And don't be shy about monitoring your teen's social media! If you see a concerning post, talk to them about what motivated them to take and post the picture. Remember: Guys lust, and girls lust to be lusted after.

If your kids are younger, it's never too early to talk about what kinds of pictures are appropriate. (We recommend reading the book *Good Pictures, Bad Pictures* with your kids.) Explain to your kids that the internet is full of pictures of body parts that God made for us to keep private. Warn them that they'll very likely encounter those pictures online. If they do, they'll probably have one of two reactions: They'll either feel embarrassed and scared to tell anyone, or they'll feel curious and want to find more pictures like that. Remind your kids that *both* reactions are normal—and the immediate, correct response is always to click away and tell a parent, teacher, or other trusted adult what they've seen and where.

KEY SCRIPTURES

We encourage you to read the following verses in context (meaning, read at least the entire chapter). Reflect on how they relate to what you're learning, and thank God for the hope and guidance found in His Word.

- Luke 4:18: "The Spirit of the Lord is upon me, because he has anointed me to proclaim good news to the poor. He has sent me to proclaim liberty to the captives and recovering of sight to the blind, to set at liberty those who are oppressed."
- Proverbs 4:23: "Keep your heart with all vigilance, for from it flow the springs of life."
- Psalm 66:16: "Come and hear, all you who fear God, and I will tell what he has done for my soul."

- Matthew 6:22-23: "The eye is the lamp of the body. So, if your eye is healthy, your whole body will be full of light, but if your eye is bad, your whole body will be full of darkness. If then the light in you is darkness, how great is the darkness!"

PAWS FOR PRAYER

In closing this chapter, reflect on what you learned in lesson 11 and journal your prayer to God here:

Praise:

Admit:

Worship with thanksgiving:

Supplication (submit your requests):

LESSON 12

Same-Sex Attraction

Hurting People to Be Loved

We have to be the generation to disciple our children to truly love and understand their same-sex-attracted peers while maintaining a commitment to biblical truth about marriage. Because…if we mess with the picture God gave us through sex, marriage, and gender, we mess with people's ability to see God accurately. Who among us is willing to stand before God and say they encouraged people to remain in bondage to a distorted view of Him when it was His desire for them to walk in freedom? We cannot afford to get this one wrong, Mama Bears.

—*Mama Bear Apologetics Guide to Sexuality and Gender Identity*, page 228

ACTIVE READING NOTES

READING FOCUS	MY RESPONSE
BEFORE YOU READ:	
After skimming the chapter title and subheads, what is one question you would like to have answered in the chapter?	My question:
WHILE YOU READ:	
List three words you discovered in the chapter in addition to the words we have provided.	My words: Book words: *false dichotomy* (page 227)— *attachment theory* (page 229)—
AFTER YOU READ:	
Did you find an answer to your pre-reading question? (We hope so.) If yes, write it down.	My answer:

List three things you highlighted or underlined in the chapter. This can be new information you learned, encouraging reinforcements of things you already knew, or just plain anything that popped out at you.	My "Aha!" moments: 1. 2. 3.

PICK A QUESTION

Use this space to review the study questions at the end of the chapter and respond to the one you find most thought-provoking or convicting.

EMPOWERING WORDS

- *Systematic theology*—The study of what the whole Bible teaches about any given topic or issue. Knowing systematic theology prevents people from forming their entire theology around a single verse taken out of context.
- *Doctrine of inerrancy*—Doctrine affirming that Scripture (in its original manuscripts) is without error, and we can trust it to accurately convey the words of God.
- *Exegesis*—The systematic study, teaching, and interpretation

of Scripture in light of its historical context, audience, and intended meaning.

- *Eisegesis*—Importing one's own personal viewpoint and using that to interpret Scripture.
- *Heteronormative*—The assumption that sexual attraction toward the opposite gender is (or should be) the norm. This word is used by trans activists and queer theorists to describe the harm and oppression caused by this assumption.

EMPOWERING THOUGHTS

Take some time to read the story of Jesus's encounter with the Samaritan woman in John 4:4-42. Keep in mind the Samaritans were a race of people the Jews utterly despised, and this woman was considered a scandalous, immoral, social outcast even to her own people. She was at the well alone—intentionally coming at a time when no one else would be there. But in that place, she met Jesus. This is a well-known story, but God's Word is so good at touching our hearts in new ways every time we go to it. As you read the story, consider the following questions:

1. How did Jesus lead with relationship (not legalism) in His encounter with this immoral woman?

2. The Samaritan woman had deep emotional needs, and she had sin in her life. Which did Jesus address first? What was her need?

3. How did the woman emotionally respond to Jesus?

4. Jesus didn't compromise truth, but who was the one to bring the Samaritan woman's sin into the conversation first?

5. How did Jesus's encounter with her affirm the Samaritan woman's value?

6. How can this story inform the way we love and relate to same-sex attracted family and friends in our own lives?

What Do We Mean by Worth and Value?

Many parents are not quite sure what to do when a child's friend or family member comes out as gay. We want to explain what is happening, but we don't want our child running to them and reminding them that they are in sin—because we are *all* in sin, honey-child. How can we as parents guide this conversation? What does it mean in practicality to treat someone with worth and value—an image bearer—who is not currently *reflecting* the *imago dei*? The main goal is to interact with them as individuals without participating (even passively) in the sin. Brainstorm the difference with your children. Playing games at recess? Interacting with someone with worth and value. Helping them ask out a same-sex crush? Participating. Make a list of activities that will promote worth and value without affirming unbiblical ideas.

DIGGING DEEPER

1. Fill in the blanks below from page 225:
   - Same-sex attraction is not the ______________ sin.
   - The gospel is not about "making ________ people ____________."
   - The gospel is about ______________________ sinners into __________ ______________________.

2. If your child comes to you saying they are gay or transgender, it is important to respond with gentleness and compassion. What are the five things we should do listed on page 227?
   -
   -
   -
   -
   -

3. Pages 227-228 discusses how people who embrace LGBTQ+ as part of God's design often end up "leaving biblical inerrancy in the dustbin as they go." Have you ever seen this happen? What do you think happens to a person's theology and faith in the long run once they deny that Scripture is God's infallible Word to humans?

4. On pages 228–230, we describe the scientific and sociological difficulties with drawing conclusions about homosexuality. Answer the following questions:

   a. Why can't we "scientifically study" a group of people if we can't clearly differentiate between the groups?

   b. According to Lisa Diamond, why are the categories of straight, gay, and bi not clear-cut? (You can see her presentation on YouTube.[1])

   c. What is the main problem with referring to someone's sexuality as an "orientation"?

   d. Someone comes to you and says that you can't change the way someone was born, and that a gay person was "born that way." According to the Lisa Diamond research, how should you respond?

5. Thought experiment: What if—one day—a gene was discovered that correlated to homosexual desires in some people? Would that change how Christians are called to behave regarding same-sex relationships according to the Bible? Why or why not?

It's Time to ROAR Like a Mother at Same-Sex Attraction

Recognize the Message

6. List and summarize the six main passages in Scripture that address homosexuality:

   a.

   b.

   c.

d.

e.

f.

7. What are the two main camps when it comes to interpreting what the Bible teaches on homosexuality?

8. How is the alternative nomenclature of "affirming" and "non-affirming" a rhetorical tactic to paint the traditional Christian view as unloving?

9. List and summarize four common arguments for Christians accepting same-sex romantic relationships as biblical (pages 233–234).

   a.

   b.

   c.

   d.

   Have you found yourself in agreement with any of these?

Offer Discernment

10. Choose two of the four lies that you hear the *most* (pages 235–236). Which ones did you choose and why? Respond to those two.

a.

b.

Argue for a Healthier Approach

11. Fill in the blank from page 236: We cannot be divided anymore. When we begin to embrace God's ________, ___________ and ____________ can begin.

12. List and summarize in one or two sentences the five important reminders on pages 236–238.

    a.

    b.

    c.

d.

e.

13. Which of the above reminders challenges you the most and why?

Reinforce with Discussion, Discipleship, and Prayer

14. In this chapter, we learned that same-sex attraction might be a symptom, not a root cause. Listening well to someone's story can help us differentiate between symptoms and root causes. Describe a situation in your life when someone listened to you well and empowered you to discern an underlying truth.

15. Review the material on the four loves in lesson 7. You can also listen to episode 97 of the *Mama Bear Apologetics Podcast*, "The Four Types of Love and Why Our Kids Need to Understand Them." Look for further opportunities this week to reinforce this concept with your kids, frequently asking them to identify which types of love they're seeing portrayed. This can even be brought into your family devotions and Bible reading. For example, in the story of the Samaritan woman at the well, what kind of love had she lived her life in service

to? What kind of love did she experience during her encounter with Jesus?

 *Whose Law Are We Talking About?*

Time for a civics lesson! On a large piece of paper, draw a Venn diagram with two overlapping circles. Label the circles *God's Law* and *Government's Law*. With your kids, name as many laws as you can think of and decide where each one should be placed. Where do God's law and civic laws overlap? Where do they differ? For instance, you might come up with "Do not murder," which would belong in the circles' shared space. Or perhaps your kids think of "drive on the right side of the road." Traffic laws would go in the government circle. This exercise can be helpful in explaining the legalization of same-sex marriage, showing your children that while same-sex marriage is legal, that doesn't mean it is approved by God.

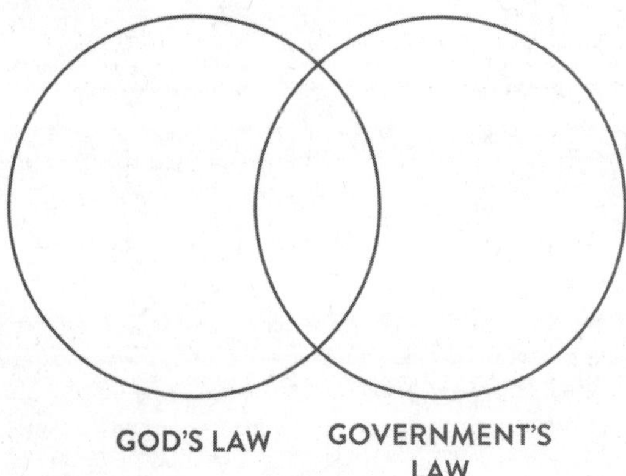

KEY SCRIPTURES

We encourage you to read the following verses in context (meaning, read at least the entire chapter). Reflect on how they relate to what you're learning, and thank God for the hope and guidance found in His Word.

- Hebrews 4:15-16: "We do not have a high priest who is unable to sympathize with our weaknesses, but one who in every respect has been tempted as we are, yet without sin. Let us then with confidence draw near to the throne of grace, that we may receive mercy and find grace to help in time of need."
- 2 Peter 2:18: "Speaking loud boasts of folly, they entice by sensual passions of the flesh those who are barely escaping from those who live in error."
- 1 Corinthians 6:11: "You were washed, you were sanctified, you were justified in the name of the Lord Jesus Christ and by the Spirit of our God."
- 2 Timothy 2:15: "Do your best to present yourself to God as one approved, a worker who has no need to be ashamed, rightly handling the word of truth."
- 1 Thessalonians 4:8: "Whoever disregards this [instruction on sexuality], disregards not man but God, who gives his Holy Spirit to you."

PAWS FOR PRAYER

In closing this chapter, reflect on what you learned in lesson 12 and journal your prayer to God here:

Praise:

Admit:

Worship with thanksgiving:

Supplication (submit your requests):

LESSON 13

I Identify as a [Fill in the Blank]

Understanding Gender Identity

How in the world can we help our kids grow into men and women of God if they aren't even sure what it means to be a man or a woman? Or if they even *are one*? Adolescents today are being taught that gender is on a spectrum and the possibilities are endless.

Gender used to be this beautiful no-brainer. It was a tiny sliver of certainty in a sea of hormonal confusion. Questioning our gender never even occurred to most of us—at least for 99.982% of us.[1] But our kids are in a different boat, and we, Mama Bears, need to be ready to counter the identity attacks being leveled at this next generation of image bearers.

—*Mama Bear Apologetics Guide to Sexuality and Gender Identity*, page 245

ACTIVE READING NOTES

READING FOCUS	MY RESPONSE
BEFORE YOU READ:	
After skimming the chapter title and subheads, what is one question you would like to have answered in the chapter?	My question:
WHILE YOU READ:	
List three words you discovered in the chapter in addition to the words we have provided.	My words: Book words: *gender identity* (page 247)— *gender expression* (page 250)— *stereotype* (page 250)— *distribution curve* (page 252)—

AFTER YOU READ:	
Did you find an answer to your pre-reading question? (We hope so.) If yes, write it down.	My answer:
List three things you highlighted or underlined in the chapter. This can be new information you learned, encouraging reinforcements of things you already knew, or just plain anything that popped out at you.	My "Aha!" moments: 1. 2. 3.

PICK A QUESTION

Use this space to review the study questions at the end of the chapter and respond to the one you find most thought-provoking or convicting.

EMPOWERING WORDS

- *Genderqueer*—A person who rejects biological gender distinctions and identifies with neither, both, or a combination of male and female genders.
- *Gender fluid*—Someone whose gender identity fluctuates instead of remaining fixed.
- *Social transition*—When an individual changes their gender presentation on the outside through their clothes, hairstyle, name, etc., and asks those around them to refer to them as another gender, but they have not had any kind of physical surgery.
- *Cisnormativity*—The assumption that identifying as one's biological gender is (or should be) the norm. This word is used by trans activists and queer theorists to describe the oppression caused by binary gender language.
- *Pronouns*—In the English language, pronouns are the short words we use so we don't have to say someone's name over and over again. Colloquially, when referring to a hypothetical person in the singular (who could be represented by a male or female equally), the pronoun *they* has sometimes been used instead of saying the hypothetical singular *he/she* over and over again. For example, a training manual might refer to a single employee, but then describe "their" duties, since the future employee might be a man or woman. This was all intended to make speaking *easier.* However, a person's pronouns have become an extension of gender expression, with trans and nonbinary people declaring that the pronouns people use for them must match their gender identity or lack of gender (as in the insistence of the pronoun *they* even when the person is not a hypothetical).

- *Neo-pronouns*—Any other words that a person has created to reflect their perceived unique gender, such as *ze/zir* or *xe/xer*. Some have gone so far as to put another noun in place of the word *self* at the end, such as *frog/frogself*.

EMPOWERING THOUGHTS

Gender roles are the social norms that reflect a particular culture's interpretation of masculinity and femininity. These societal "rules" can be quite different depending upon where and when someone lives. Most of us can agree that *some* of these standards are arbitrary and have led to overly confining expectations for men and women throughout history. Fast-forward to Western culture today, and gender itself is being defined as the internal sense of self as female, male, both, or neither—basically what someone feels they are based upon these stereotypes. Reflecting on the discussion of *identity* on pages 128–131, why might basing one's gender on shifting cultural stereotypes lead to confusion rather than clarity?

Two trends you might not be aware of are Christian kids identifying as bisexual or nonbinary. These two identities allow them to be a part of the LGBTQ+ community while technically retaining their cisgender heterosexual practices. First, be aware that this is happening in your community. Second, equip yourself to respond to it—and prepare your kids for the peer pressure to participate. A kid who is prepared for peer pressure is less likely to fall for it.

DIGGING DEEPER

1. Having a label or disorder is almost considered a "badge of honor" among this new generation. Have you noticed this? List three "labels"

(personality type, sexual orientation, gender identity, or mental illness or disability) that you've noticed kids overidentifying with.

2. How might identifying *as* a certain personality, or certain disorder, impede people's efforts at obedience to God's commands? (Example: I'm an introvert, so I don't need to be sharing the gospel or spending time with people.) What do you think is the difference between using personality knowledge to *understand* oneself (and one's tendencies) as opposed to using it to *excuse* oneself from doing uncomfortable things? (Bonus points: If you have the first *Mama Bear Apologetics* book on cultural lies, look at the linguistically stolen word *authentic* as it relates it to this question. See pages 72–74 in that book.)

3. Read pages 248–249. Why did the feminists push back on the idea of women's roles? Did they have a legitimate point? Are there any ways you think they might have taken it too far? (For more on this, see chapter 14 in *Mama Bear Apologetics: Empowering Your Kids to Challenge Cultural Lies*.)

4. Complete this sentence from page 250: Gender stereotypes ____________________ many but _______________________ none.

   Unpack this statement in your own words:

5. Explain the following concepts:

   a. What is a distribution curve?

   b. What does the height of a distribution curve tell us in terms of what is "normal"? How is normal defined in terms of a distribution curve?

   c. How do overlapping distribution curves explain *general* gender differences?

   d. Diagram the following scenario on an overlapping male and female distribution curve: David loves to dance and isn't crazy about football. Mark where he might put himself in the graphs on the next page:

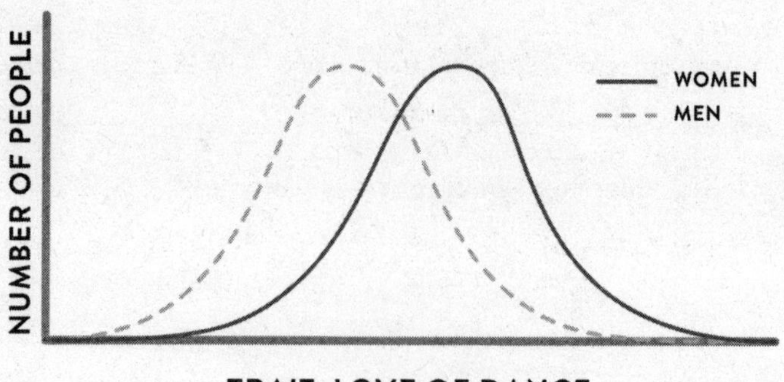

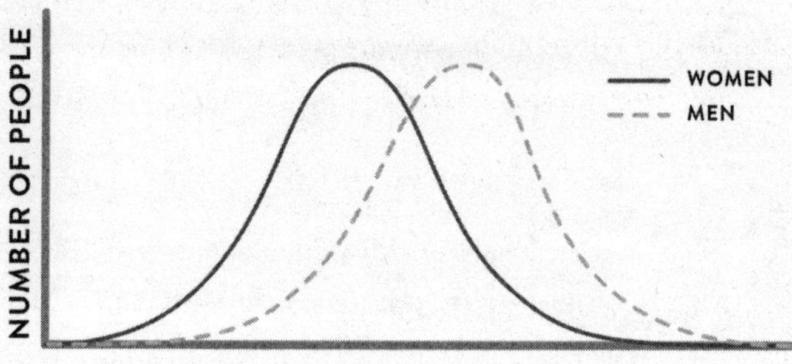

e. What would this same graph look like if a gender theorist were using the two-dimensional spectrum? Where would David fall on this graph and what might he conclude about his gender identity using this two-dimensional spectrum?

   Put a dot where you think David would fall on the graphs.

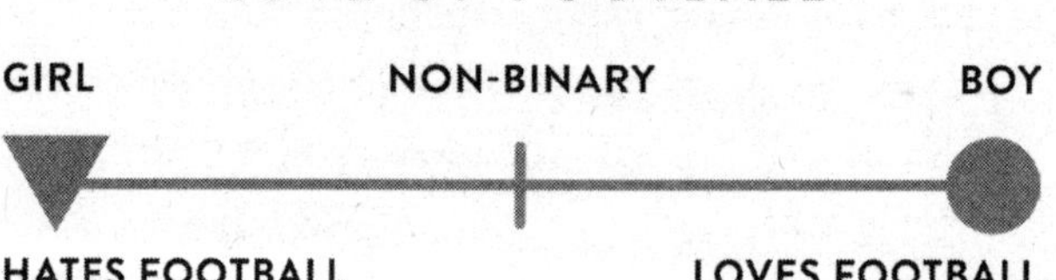

LOVE OF DANCE

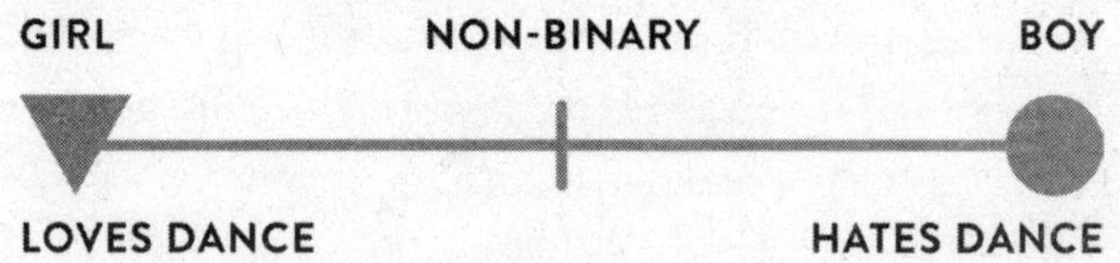

f. Now let's make it personal. Pick an interest, personality trait, or aptitude where you fall outside of the "gender norm." Draw what you think the graph might look like for men and women and where you land. Practice explaining to someone how the graph works, and how there is room for men and women on each curve no matter where they land.

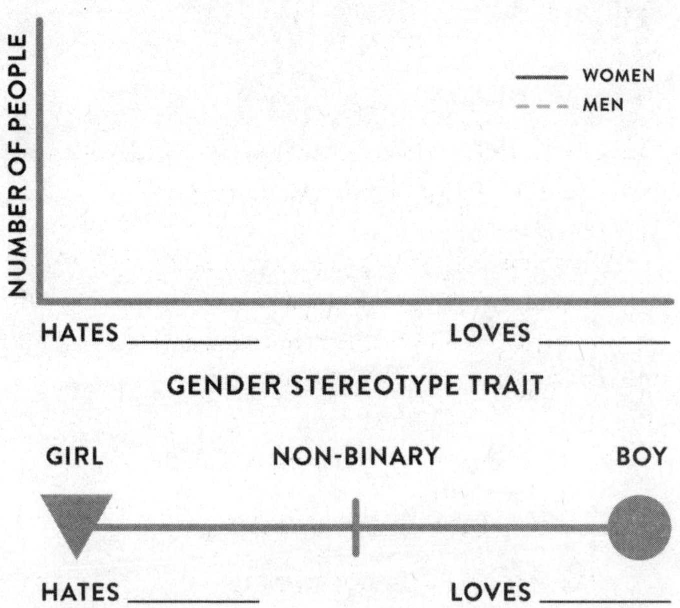

g. What would this same graph look like if a gender theorist were using the two-dimensional spectrum? Where would David fall on this graph and what might he conclude about his gender identity using this two-dimensional spectrum?

6. Read Proverbs 31:10-31. This description of the "wife of noble character" is considered the biblical epitome of womanhood. In what ways does the Proverbs 31 woman match what we think of as female gender stereotypes? In what ways does she defy female stereotypes? What is she most praised for? (Hint: 1 Samuel 16:7)

It's Time to ROAR Like a Mother at Gender Identity

Recognize the Message

7. List the four main messages found on pages 256–257.

   •

   •

   •

   •

8. What problems could you foresee with "trying out all the (sexuality

and gender) identities to see what fits you" advice? In what ways could following this advice open doors you can't close?

 *Perception or Reality?*

Remember the discussion on desensitization in lesson 8? One thing that's being repeated to our kids from kindergarten to college—not to mention in the media—is that gender identity and biological sex can be different. This has been repeated so many times that our children accept it as true—just because it's so familiar. This is equating perception with reality. Discuss with your children how our feelings don't always line up with reality, no matter how strongly they are felt. *This* is the message we need to be repeating to our kids ad nauseum. See maxim 7 on page 305 for help.

Offer Discernment

9. List two personal takeaways from the discussion of what Christians can learn from what modern gender theorists get right on pages 257–258.

10. Rephrase each of the lies from pages 258–260 in your own words. Which lie have you encountered most frequently? How might you teach your children to respond to this lie?

    •

    •

•

•

Argue for a Healthier Approach

11. There is so much confusion in our world regarding what it means to be a man or a woman. Which of the three ways the Bible addresses this (pages 260–261) do you believe is hardest for today's youth to accept or understand? Why?

12. Take 60 seconds to write out as many gender stereotypes as you can for women, and then do the same for men. How many of these stereotypes can be reduced to an interest, an aptitude, or a personality type?

Reinforce with Discussion, Discipleship, and Prayer

13. Ideologies are about truth claims, while people are individuals with their own needs, wants, and opinions. Sometimes Christians hesitate to befriend people with unbiblical beliefs because they worry their kindness will be confused with agreement. Talk to your kids about the difference between loving a person and agreeing with their beliefs.

What's the goal of showing God's love to people with whom we disagree? (Hint: Romans 2:4)

14. Proponents of gender theory often target kids who feel they don't fit in. Ask your kids to describe a time when they felt out of place. What could someone have done to make them feel more included? Use that memory to help them identify someone specific in their school or youth group who might feel the same. Create a plan for them to offer the same kindness they had wanted. Follow up with them to hear how it is going!

15. On the flip side, sometimes being too comfortable with people of differing ideologies can reveal what someone truly believes. Pay attention to who your kids feel they "fit in" with the most. While Jesus showed love for "tax collectors and sinners," they weren't part of His inner circle like the disciples were (Matthew 9:10-12). We shouldn't limit friendships to those who believe like we do, but our best friends (and those of our kids) should be people on a similar faith journey (Proverbs 27:17). What criteria do you use to discern who is appropriate for your inner circle? (One Mama Bear I know refuses to be besties with women who trash talk their husbands.) How can you help your kids identify their own age-appropriate criteria?

KEY SCRIPTURES

We encourage you to read the following verses (meaning, read at least the entire chapter). Reflect on how they relate to what you're learning, and thank God for the hope and guidance found in His Word.

- Psalm 139:13: "You formed my inward parts; you knitted me together in my mother's womb."
- Job 33:4: "The Spirit of God has made me, and the breath of the Almighty gives me life."
- Micah 6:8: "He has told you, O man, what is good; and what does the LORD require of you but to do justice, and to love kindness, and to walk humbly with your God?"
- Romans 6:6-7: "Our old self was crucified with him in order that the body of sin might be brought to nothing, so that we would no longer be enslaved to sin. For one who has died has been set free from sin."

PAWS FOR PRAYER

In closing this chapter, reflect on what you learned in lesson 13 and journal your prayer to God here:

Praise:

Admit:

Worship with thanksgiving:

Supplication (submit your requests):

LESSON 14

*Trans*cending the Gender Cult

When Birds Identify as Bees

A disproportionately large amount of political discourse has focused on mainstreaming what used to be a fraction of one percent of the population. This group is now so "protected" that they are virtually untouchable. Say anything remotely critical of the LGBTQ+ ideology, and you'll be labeled a hateful bigot. It's like a cult! Okay, maybe not "like" a cult; it *is* a cult—with all the tell-tale signs...Cults prey upon people who are hurting because they are more vulnerable to being manipulated by the promise of clarity and relief...Once a cult has found (or created) a person who is disoriented, hurting, and confused, they draw them in with extravagant displays of affirmation and acceptance. *You finally belong! We're your family! You are one of us!* The feeling of "unconditional" acceptance is the proverbial carrot that keeps the recruit coming back time after time, no matter how abusive the cult becomes...Once a recruit becomes a full-blown member, the cult does what all cults do—demands total obedience with a zero-tolerance policy for critique. Step out of line, and the member will be slandered, disciplined, or even disfellowshipped. Listen to any detransition story and you'll hear about how quickly the person's "glitter family" rejected them as soon as they began questioning their transition. And by now, the member has cut all ties with anyone outside the cult, making it much harder to leave.

—*Mama Bear Apologetics Guide to Sexuality and Gender Identity*, pages 266, 267, 268 and 269

ACTIVE READING NOTES

READING FOCUS	MY RESPONSE
BEFORE YOU READ:	
After skimming the chapter title and subheads, what is one question you would like to have answered in the chapter?	My question:
WHILE YOU READ:	
List three words you discovered in the chapter in addition to the words we have provided.	My words: Book words: *love-bomb* (page 268)— *SRY gene* (page 274)— *intersex* (page 275)—
AFTER YOU READ:	
Did you find an answer to your pre-reading question? (We hope so.) If yes, write it down.	My answer:

List three things you highlighted or underlined in the chapter. This can be new information you learned, encouraging reinforcements of things you already knew, or just plain anything that popped out at you.	My "Aha!" moments: 1. 2. 3.

PICK A QUESTION

Use this space to review the study questions at the end of the chapter and respond to the one you find most thought-provoking or convicting.

EMPOWERING WORDS

- *Cult*—A group comprised of people with religious-like devotion to a set of unusual beliefs or extreme ideologies whereby conformity to the group leader or dogma allows no room for questioning and often encourages adherents to cut ties with those outside the cult.
- *Deprogramming*—The process whereby brainwashed cult members unlearn the harmful beliefs they adopted while in the cult.
- *Gender confirmation surgery (GCS)*—The surgical component of transitioning. "Top surgery" refers to either removing or

augmenting breast tissue, and "bottom surgery" refers to genital reconstruction to match the desired gender.

- *Gender-affirming therapy*—Treatment that focuses on prioritizing a person's self-perceived gender identity over their biological sex.

EMPOWERING THOUGHTS

Because we live in a post-fall world, we must acknowledge that feelings of dysphoria, dissatisfaction, or disassociation with one's biological sex is a real problem that makes a real impact on the lives of many people. As Christians, we also know that most of the treatments our culture presents for this problem are not in line with God's design for our bodies or our minds and, as such, do not provide long-term relief. Our desire is for people to live in freedom, and freedom will never be found when we go against how we were designed because *we cannot flourish in what we weren't created for.* Yes, the person may experience a false peace when they finally give in to sin and brokenness. They may even feel as though they are finally flourishing! But it is not true flourishing because it betrays what their mind, body, and spirit were created for.

As the number of people transitioning increases, it's becoming more and more likely that we will find ourselves in conversations with people who are detransitioning or questioning their transition. Without compromising our convictions, we must have compassion for their pain and a heart of graciousness toward the challenges they face, no matter how foreign their situation may seem to us. We want to demonstrate our care for them by listening to their stories and by offering them truth that results in real, lasting peace. But remember, first establish a real relationship before diving into worldview surgery.

1. When it comes to discussing the topic of gender identity and transgenderism, do you find yourself feeling angry, confused, squeamish,

or condescending? How do you think your innate response impacts your ability to love on those who are struggling?

2. It can be difficult for some people to distinguish between a harmful movement like gender ideology and the individuals who have fallen prey to this movement's teachings. List five ways that you can purposefully love someone who is struggling without affirming their ideology.

   •
   •
   •
   •
   •

3. When it comes to the issue of transgenderism and individuals who identify as transgender, are you someone who is inclined to have too much compassion or not enough? (In other words, are you more like the "terrifying truth teller" or the "compassionate compromiser"?) What are the dangers to your witness and the gospel message if you err too far in either direction?

4. What role does this gender ideology currently play in your child's life? (Answers will vary depending on where you live, how old your child is, what their schooling situation is, and what kind of media you allow in your home.) Do you feel prepared to respond to it? Why or why not?

DIGGING DEEPER

Complete the following chart regarding cults and gender theory (pages 266–269).

CULT TACTIC	HOW IT WORKS

CULT TACTIC	HOW IT WORKS

1. How does each of the following traits contribute to gender confusion?

   - Neurodivergence:

   - Intellectual giftedness:

   - Co-occurring mood or psychiatric disorder:

- Prior trauma:

- Early porn exposure:

2. What is the difference between the terms *dysphoria* and *disorder*? How has this change in terminology changed the way we therapeutically treat people? (See pages 271–272.)

3. Compare and contrast Classic Gender Identity Disorder with Rapid-Onset Gender Dysphoria. What are the main criteria for identifying each of them? (See pages 273–274.)

4. Why do you think adopting the label *nonbinary* is so attractive to our kids (and especially Christian kids)? (Pay attention to page 274.)

5. Consider the following logical vignette. How have you seen this logic playing out in society? (Think especially in terms of the assumption first and drag culture second.)

   A: Gender is what you do.

   FC: I can change what I do.

   C: Therefore, I can change my gender.

6. What is the short answer for what science shows about gender? (See page 276.)

7. Summarize what you learned about the role of biology in the formation of gender. (See pages 274–276.)

   SRY gene ______________________________

   ____

   testosterone ______________________________

   ____

8. In one sentence, what does the Bible say about transgenderism and gender expression? (See Deuteronomy 22:5.)

9. The subject of gender and gender identity has become a massive cultural conversation, and there's a lot of misinformation out there that even informed Christians can unwittingly absorb. This chapter is a great starting point. Write out any questions or uncertainties you still have about this topic:

   -
   -
   -
   -
   -

   How can you go about answering these questions?

KEY SCRIPTURES

We encourage you to read the following verses in context (meaning, read at least the entire chapter). Reflect on how they relate to what you're learning, and thank God for the hope and guidance found in His Word.

- Matthew 18:6: "If anyone causes one of these little ones—those who believe in me—to stumble, it would be better for them to have a large millstone hung around their neck and to be drowned in the depths of the sea" (NIV).
- Proverbs 22:5-6: "In the paths of the wicked are snares and pitfalls, but those who would preserve their life stay far from them. Start children off on the way they should go, and even when they are old they will not turn from it" (NIV).

- Philippians 1:9-11: "This is my prayer: that your love may abound more and more in knowledge and depth of insight, so that you may be able to discern what is best and may be pure and blameless for the day of Christ, filled with the fruit of righteousness that comes through Jesus Christ—to the glory and praise of God" (NIV).
- Romans 16:17: "Watch out for those who cause divisions and put obstacles in your way that are contrary to the teaching you have learned. Keep away from them" (NIV).

PAWS FOR PRAYER

In closing this chapter, reflect on what you learned in lesson 14 and journal your prayer to God here:

Praise:

Admit:

Worship with thanksgiving:

Supplication (submit your requests):

LESSON 15

Taking Up Your Sexual Cross

Because We're All Born This Way

The call to discipleship with Jesus is a heavy one, and we shouldn't pretend otherwise with our kids. In Luke 9:23-24, Jesus says to His disciples, "Whoever wants to be my disciple must deny themselves and take up their cross daily and follow me. For whoever wants to save their life will lose it, but whoever loses their life for me will save it" (NIV). Here, Jesus is saying bluntly that the Christian walk will not be an easy one; we'll all have burdens to bear. Is this scary? Yup. Do we know what crosses we'll be called to carry in our own individual lives? Nope. Do we know what crosses our *children* will be called to carry? Also, no. So what can we know?...Sexual holiness is itself a cross we will have to carry—each one of us.

—*Mama Bear Apologetics Guide to Sexuality and Gender Identity*, pages 291, 292

ACTIVE READING NOTES

READING FOCUS	MY RESPONSE
BEFORE YOU READ:	
After skimming the chapter title and subheads, what is one question you would like to have answered in the chapter?	My question:
WHILE YOU READ:	
List three words you discovered in the chapter in addition to the words we have provided.	My words: Book words: *encouragement* (page 290)— *imminent* (page 298)—
AFTER YOU READ:	
Did you find an answer to your pre-reading question? (We hope so.) If yes, write it down.	My answer:

List three things you highlighted or underlined in the chapter. This can be new information you learned, encouraging reinforcements of things you already knew, or just plain anything that popped out at you.	My "Aha!" moments: 1. 2. 3.

PICK A QUESTION

Use this space to review the study questions at the end of the chapter and respond to the one you find most thought-provoking or convicting.

EMPOWERING WORDS

- *Sacrifice*—The act of offering to God something deeply precious at personal cost.
- *Contempt*—When we feel that someone or something is worthless, beneath consideration, or deserving scorn.
- *Humility*—An accurate view of oneself grounded in who you are in Christ, so secure in God's love for you that you are willing to serve and sacrifice. Humility means not thinking too much or too little—not too highly or too lowly—of oneself or others.

EMPOWERING THOUGHTS

Christians are called to take up their crosses. Some people see crosses as simply hardships—"thorns in the flesh" they are called to endure in life. This is only partly true. A real cross to bear involves something more than trial and tribulation; taking up a cross means being *obedient and faithful even when the situation is unfair.* That is what distinguishes trials from crosses.

Many false gospels out there promise you your best life now through health, wealth, and prosperity. (We wrote about several of those in the first *Mama Bear Apologetics* book.) There are many false Jesuses out there who look more like personal assistants or authenticity coaches than the King of kings and Lord of lords. None of these prepares us for real life as a Christ-follower. None of these offers eternal hope, healing, and freedom from the pain of this world.

1. What are some of the empty, powerless, false messages you have heard recently from culture or even the church, especially on suffering?

2. Do these messages reflect *reality*? Explain how these messages discourage rather than encourage people (pages 289–290).

3. Read 2 Corinthians 11:23-33. List a few of the things Paul describes happening in his life.

4. Give one example of a popular "encouragement" that would fall utterly flat on Paul's ears.

How might a proper understanding of *encouragement* affect what you choose to read or listen to? What you post online? What do you think of apologists who seek to lovingly warn the church of deception?

DIGGING DEEPER

1. On page 297, we learn that we don't get to decide the right thing based on what's fair. How did Jesus model this in His earthly ministry?

2. Summarize the ten crosses explained in the chapter (pages 292–297).

CROSS TO BEAR	WAYS TO BE FAITHFUL DESPITE AN UNFAIR SITUATION

CROSS TO BEAR	WAYS TO BE FAITHFUL DESPITE AN UNFAIR SITUATION

3. Do you (or someone you know) carry any of these crosses? How has it affected you or your loved ones?

4. Do you feel a ministerial call to individuals carrying any of these particular crosses? If so, which one(s)? Why?

5. Choose one or two crosses and share some ideas on how we as the Church might more effectively help carry them.

 *How Well Do We Know Our Neighbor's Cross?*

Jesus calls us to take up our cross and follow Him. We take up our cross when we live with trials and tribulations and remain joyfully faithful to God. Consider a faithful member of your church community—someone well-known to your family. With this person's permission, or perhaps with their help (depending on your relationship), share with your children some of the crosses this person bears. Perhaps that carefree choir member who is celebrating 10 years sober, or the woman who joyfully serves despite struggling with chronic health conditions.

Help your children understand that all Christians carry crosses. Adverse circumstances, burdens, and trials can make obedience hard, but we are called to faithfulness despite our unique difficulties. Establish in your kids' minds that our Lord does not always lift the cross off our backs; rather He shapes us through them as we submit to Him, carrying it like He did. We do not have a high priest who is unable to sympathize with our weaknesses (Hebrews 4:15). Rather, He carried His cross first so that we could follow His example. And like Simon of Cyrene, sometimes our job is to help others to carry their unique crosses (Matthew 27:32).

 *Carrying Each Other's Burdens*

Encourage your children to ask their friends what struggles they undergo, and ask them how those struggles affect their friends' lives. Teach your children to familiarize themselves with the struggles of others—and teach them to ask, "How can I help you carry this burden? How can I support you and help you remain faithful in this situation?"

One way to teach this to your kids? Model it! When your children have unfair circumstances that make their lives more difficult, ask them how you can help them do the right thing. What does faithfulness mean in an unfair situation? Sometimes helping them carry their cross means listening to them, crying with them, or praising them for their acts of faithfulness, no matter how small.

KEY SCRIPTURES

We encourage you to read the following verses in context (meaning, read at least the entire chapter). Reflect on how they relate to what you're learning, and thank God for the hope and guidance found in His Word.

- 2 Corinthians 1:3-4: "Blessed be the God and Father of our Lord Jesus Christ, the Father of mercies and God of all comfort, who comforts us in all our affliction, so that we may be able to comfort those who are in any affliction, with the comfort with which we ourselves are comforted by God."
- Psalm 55:22: "Cast your burden on the Lord, and he will sustain you; he will never permit the righteous to be moved."
- Matthew 11:29: "Take my yoke upon you, and learn from me, for I am gentle and lowly in heart, and you will find rest for your souls."
- Romans 12:10: "Love one another with brotherly affection. Outdo one another in showing honor."
- 1 John 4:12: "No one has ever seen God; if we love one another, God abides in us and his love is perfected in us."

PAWS FOR PRAYER

In closing this chapter, reflect on what you learned in lesson 15 and journal your prayer to God here:

Praise:

Admit:

Worship with thanksgiving:

Supplication (submit your requests):

Notes

Lesson 5: Are You Sex-Smarter than a Fifth Grader?

1. In one video titled "Am I Ready to Have Sex?" one of the "important questions" kids should ask themselves is: "Do I actually know anyone I'd like to have sex with?" See around the 40-second mark here: https://www.youtube.com/watch?v=rj3wBPZjy-8.

Lesson 6: The Enemy's New Playbook

1. For a broader discussion of these tactics, see Gabriele Kuby, *The Global Sexual Revolution: Destruction of Freedom in the Name of Freedom* (LifeSite, 2015).

Lesson 7: The Genderbread Person

1. "Genderbread Person & LGBTQ Umbrella," The Safe Zone Project, http://thesafezoneproject.com/wp-content/uploads/2015/08/GenderbreadPersonLGBTQUmbrella.pdf.

Lesson 9: Queer Theory

1. Furscience, "What's a Furry?," updated February 9, 2021, https://furscience.com/whats-a-furry/. Therian-Guide.com, "An Updated Alter-Human Term List," https://forums.therian-guide.com/Thread-An-updated-Alter-Human-Term-List.
2. Amber Roberts, "Otherkin Are People Too; They Just Identify as Nonhuman," Vice, July 16, 2015, https://www.vice.com/en/article/mvxgwa/from-dragons-to-foxes-the-otherkin-community-believes-you-can-be-whatever-you-want-to-be.

Lesson 10: Purity Culture

1. Linda Kay Klein, *Pure: Inside the Evangelical Movement that Shamed a Generation of Young Women and How I Broke Free* (Touchstone, 2018). This happened in Klein's small-town church, and she implied that all evangelical churches were the same.
2. *Strong's Lexicon*, "*kosmios*," Bible Hub, accessed February 28, 2025, https://biblehub.com/greek/2887.htm.

Lesson 12: Same-Sex Attraction

1. Lisa Diamond, "Lisa Diamond on Sexual Fluidity of Men and Women," YouTube, December 6, 2013, www.youtube.com/watch?feature=player_embedded&v=m2rTHDOuUBw.

Lesson 13: Gender Identity

1. True intersex conditions that leave the gender of an individual ambiguous account for only about 0.018% of the population. Leonard Sax, "How Common Is Intersex? A Response to Anne Fausto-Sterling," *The Journal of Sex Research*, no. 39 (2002), 174–178, doi: 10.1080/00224490209552139.

About the Authors

HILLARY MORGAN FERRER is the founder and president of Mama Bear Apologetics. She feels a burden for providing accessible apologetics resources for busy moms. She is the chief author and editor of the bestselling books *Mama Bear Apologetics: Empowering Your Kids to Challenge Cultural Lies* and *Honest Prayers for Mama Bears.* Hillary has her master's degree in biology and loves helping moms to discern truths and lies in culture from both a biblical and scientific perspective. She is passionate about understanding the root causes of doubt and helping people identify the sources of their barriers to faith. Hillary and her husband, John, have been married since 2007 and minister together as an apologetics team.

TEASI CANNON is a wife, mother, teacher, author, and contributor to the Mama Bear Apologetics ministry. Her passion for discipleship led her to obtain a master's degree in pastoral counseling from Liberty Theological Seminary. Teasi lives in Tennessee with her husband, Bill. They have three amazing grown children, a fantastic son-in-law, a beautiful daughter-in-law, and several precious grandbabies.

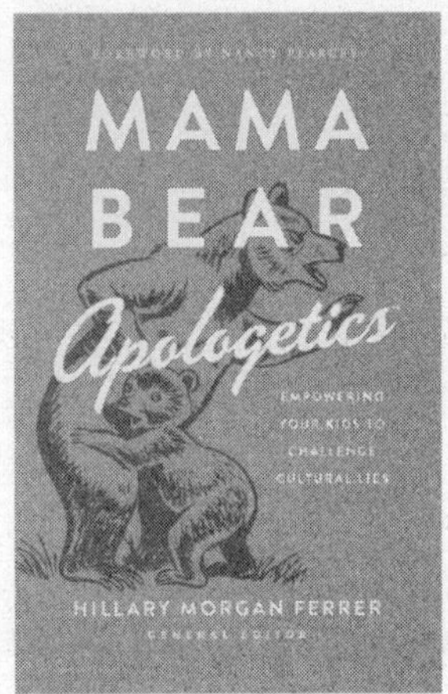

MAMA BEAR APOLOGETICS

#RoarLikeAMother

The problem with lies is they don't often sound like lies. They seem harmless, and even sound *right.* So what's a Mama Bear to do when her kids seem to be absorbing the culture's lies uncritically?

Mama Bear Apologetics® is the book you've been looking for. This mom-to-mom guide will equip you to teach your kids how to form their own biblical beliefs about what is true and what is false. Through transparent life stories and clear, practical applications—including prayer strategies—this band of Mama Bears offers you tools to train yourself, so you can turn around and train your kids.

Are you ready to answer the rallying cry, "Mess with our kids and we will demolish your arguments"? Join the Mama Bears and raise your voice to protect your kids—by teaching them how to think through and address the issues head-on, yet with gentleness and respect.

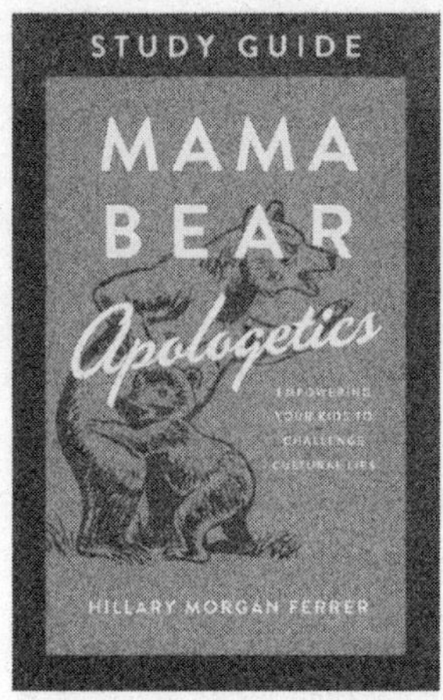

MAMA BEAR APOLOGETICS STUDY GUIDE

Calling All Mama (and Papa) Bears!

When your kids come home from school asking questions about everything from moral relativity to cultural Marxism to whether God even exists, you need to be prepared with biblically sound answers. With this user-friendly companion to the bestselling book *Mama Bear Apologetics*®, you'll understand the secular worldviews your children face every day and build the foundation of faith and knowledge you need to equip them to respond to culture's lies.

Perfect for individual or group study, this study guide will help you…

- examine more thoroughly the issues facing your children, and analyze them from a biblical perspective
- discover practical ways to empower your kids with God's wisdom for cultural challenges
- counter nonbiblical viewpoints with truth, love, kindness, and respect

Knowing what is true is the best way to argue against what is false. The *Mama Bear Apologetics® Study Guide* will ready you to be confident as you seek effective ways to help your kids stand strong.

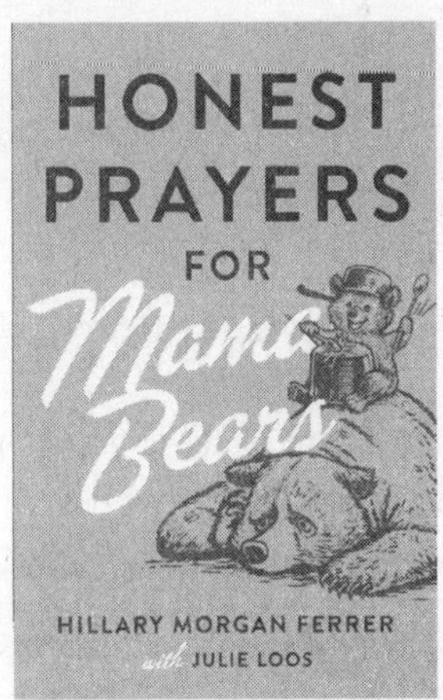

HONEST PRAYERS FOR MAMA BEARS

Encouragement to Pray What You Really Feel

In the everyday battle of raising kids who love Jesus while living in a world that doesn't, God invites you to come to Him. No cleaning up, no pretenses, no fancy words—all you need is to tell Him what's truly on your heart and then ask for the wisdom, encouragement, and protection that only He can provide.

From the bestselling team behind *Mama Bear Apologetics®* comes a one-of-a-kind book of prayers gathered from mamas just like you, speaking to the spectrum of seasons, concerns, and needs faced throughout Christian motherhood. You will become more vulnerable and intentional in your conversations with God as you pray in specific and timely ways for your family, your community, and even for yourself.

Honest Prayers for Mama Bears puts words to the cries of your heart as you seek clarity and truth in today's confused culture. Through these praises, confessions, thanksgivings, and petitions, you'll lay your burdens at your heavenly Father's feet and experience His comfort and hope as you entrust Him with your unedited thoughts.

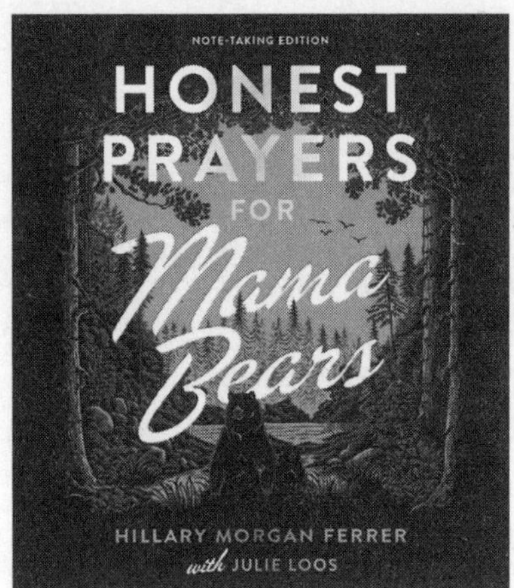

HONEST PRAYERS FOR MAMA BEARS NOTE-TAKING EDITION

From the bestselling team behind *Mama Bear Apologetics*® comes a one-of-a-kind book of prayers gathered from mamas just like you. Now with space on each page for personal reflection, this beautiful hardcover note-taking edition encourages you to pray what you really feel—and grow deeper in intimacy with God each day.

This book puts words to the cries of your heart as you seek clarity and truth in today's confused culture. With ample journaling space on each page, this special keepsake edition will allow you to return to your praises, confessions, thanksgivings, and petitions throughout the years, helping you see how God has continually guided you and your family. Experience His comfort and hope as you entrust Him with your unedited thoughts.